CW00537614

MELBOURNE

A CITY OF VILLAGES

STORIES PAST AND PRESENT

MELBOURNE
A CITY OF VILLAGES

DALE CAMPISI
PHOTOGRAPHY BY BRADY MICHAELS

hardie grant books
MELBOURNE · LONDON

CONTENTS

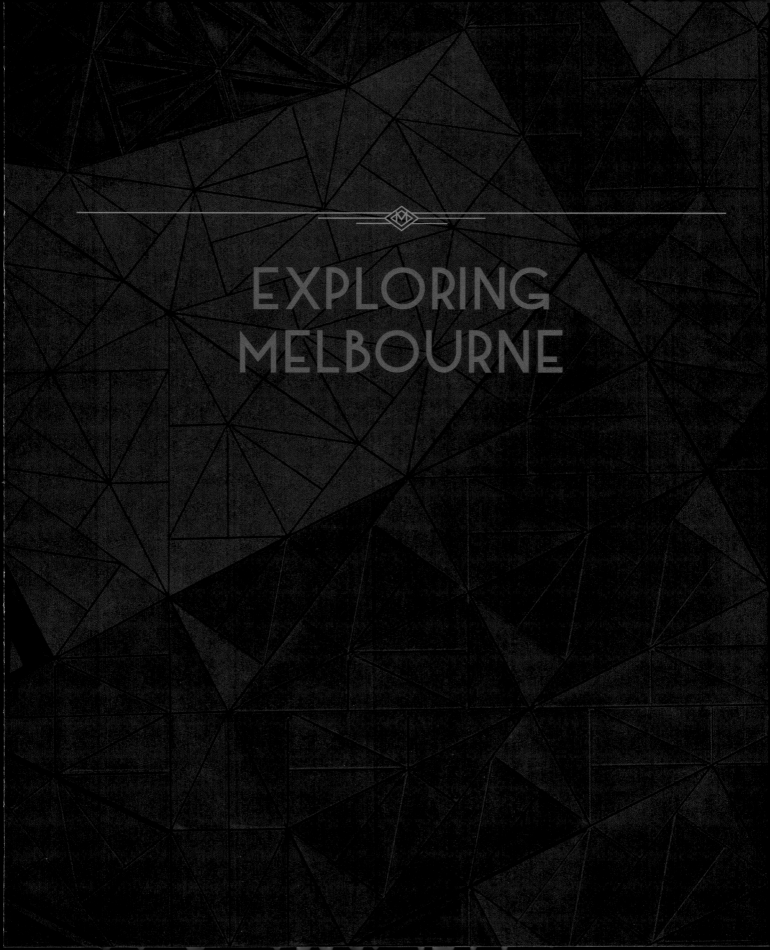

EXPLORING
MELBOURNE

LIKE SO MANY Melburnians, I'm an immigrant to this city. I was born in country Victoria but have spent most of my adult life here. I've lived all over the city and in all types of buildings: from Gordon House on Little Bourke Street to Temple Court on Collins Street, a stables in Carlton to a Californian Bungalow in Camberwell, and in Northcote, North Melbourne, Brunswick and Prahran. Even Glen Iris. Yes, I still have to go west.

It's a fascinating city, wherever you live. And you can read this city's history if you know where to look. From architecture to landscaping to infrastructure to public monuments to the faces of people on the street, Melbourne is a city that wears its history. This book is my view of how and why Melbourne was shaped and became the Melbourne it is today.

Historian Jenny Lee introduced me to the idea that Melbourne is a city of villages; but these days it can be hard to see the villages for the metropolis. My Melbourne covers inner Melbourne, which more or less reflects the extent of Marvellous Melbourne in the 1880s, including the city's long established hillside and seaside destinations. I'm constantly in search of Melbourne's pre-contact history, but this book is ostensibly about Melbourne and its people since 1835.

Part guidebook, part history primer, this book visits 50 historic villages and uses significant sites to tell Melbourne's stories. Inside you'll read about how convict William Buckley escaped to live with local Aboriginal people for 32 years, how John Batman discovered a little turning basin in the Yarra River in 1835, where Madame Brussels ran her notorious brothel, and where Kylie Minogue grew up. About trams, little penguins, markets, laneways, a drive-in and South Melbourne dim sims. From Williamstown to Werribee, Sandridge to Sorrento, Brighton to Box Hill, this book tells of influences from England, Italy, Vietnam, America and many other countries whose people came to this city to build new lives and thus added to the richness of the city.

Melbourne's villages spread out from the city for a 20 kilometre radius and beyond. The Yarra and Port Phillip have defined and influenced Melbourne, and so too has surveyor Robert Hoddle's famous grid of streets. During the land boom of the 1870s and 1880s, when Melbourne was among the richest cities in the world, developer-politicians cultivated the city's growth, conspiring to create a railway system that reached out in every direction from the tightly woven grid of the inner city – and reap the benefits of inflated land prices. Known as the

Octopus Act, it fed the land boom – and Thomas Bent, the Act's creator and a private developer, benefitted enormously. The railway extension from Caulfield to Cheltenham in 1883 even gave us the suburb Bentleigh, developed by Bent himself. Pubs and post offices, butchers, grocers, banks, clothiers and confectioners all blossomed in proximity to train stations. Manufacturing too. Along with schools these businesses anchor neighbourhoods. Residents give them their flavour. There are the Chinese who have commanded Little Bourke Street since the gold rush, the Italians of Lygon Street, the Vietnamese of Victoria Street, the Jews of Caulfield, and the Middle Eastern people of Sydney Road. Then there are the multicultural melting pots of Footscray, Box Hill and Dandenong. As always, the rich favour the hills to the east; the poorer gather on the flats, and increasingly, on the periphery of the city.

The spectacular view from the balcony of the Shrine of Remembrance. **PREVIOUS PAGES** *(left) A bird's eye view of Melbourne, circa 1886; (right) The distinctive geometric patterns of Federation Square.*

Today, cafes, restaurants, pubs and bars are central to the life of our villages, each with its own historical, social and cultural influences. Effectively built around the university, Carlton is the intellectual home of Melbourne, with its famous bookshop, arthouse cinema and alternative theatre. Working class Fitzroy went bohemian in the 1970s and is today renowned for its cafes, bars, restaurants and other entertainments. Adjacent Collingwood is edgier, with a strong gay community. Richmond is still hard to pin down, South Yarra remains flashy and St Kilda – perhaps the city's best known suburb aside from the fictional Erinsborough in *Neighbours* – now teems with backpackers, as Brunswick does with hipsters. Portsea is still a private holiday destination for the elite, and Melbourne's inner eastern enclave of suburbs is known for its private schools. Werribee and Melton in the outer west are among the fastest-growing regions in the whole country, and the Dandenong Ranges still delight day-trippers with its winding roads, bush walks and scenic railway.

There's a lot to explore in Melbourne's past and present. Let's take a look.

Dale Campisi

OPPOSITE The Rialto Towers soar high above the old Rialto, and mirror the city's weather with reflective glass.

MELBOURNE NOW

MELBOURNE IS REGARDED as one of the world's most liveable cities and the term 'Marvellous Melbourne' – first used in the 1880s – is still frequently used by its residents and in the media.

Covering 9,000 square kilometres, Melbourne is an enormous city. The Yarra River, the very reason why Melbourne is where it is, weaves its way through the city and suburbs, at the centre of our everyday lives, even if only subconsciously. Since the 2000s, the city has sustained the highest population increase and economic growth rate of any Australian capital city, but at 4.3 million people it's not exactly high density. The urban boundary continues to expand, but with progress comes renewal and old industrial centres such as at Southbank, Docklands and Port Melbourne, have been transformed.

Melbourne is a place of abundance. The local Indigenous peoples lived in perfect harmony with the land, working only about 30 hours a week to sustain themselves. European squatters and their sheep quickly changed how Melbourne's land was used, but it was the gold rush of the 1850s that built the Marvellous Melbourne we know today. It first emerged in grand civic buildings in the central business district (CBD), but you can see the wealth of the gold rush at its most ostentatious in the mansions of the wealthy squatters and land boomers in suburbs such as Brighton, St Kilda, Toorak and Kew – still some of Melbourne's most affluent suburbs.

Waves of immigrants have flooded Melbourne's ports throughout its short European history. In the 1830s early settlers came from Van Diemen's Land (now Tasmania) in search of pasture, then in the 1850s they came from all over the world in search of gold. Economic, political and social refugees from around the world followed both world wars and hardships since, first from Europe, more recently from South-East Asia, Africa and the Middle East, and presumably more will come from the Pacific in the years to come. Melbourne today is a proudly multicultural place: about a quarter of Melburnians were born overseas, and there are particularly large communities of Italians, Vietnamese, Chinese, Greeks and Indians.

Melbourne is one of Asia-Pacific's leading financial centres. The city's diversified economy ranges from finance to manufacturing, education to tourism. Numerous corporate giants maintain their headquarters here, including BHP Billiton, the world's largest mining company; Sigma and CSL, two of the world's largest pharmaceutical companies; and NAB and ANZ, two of Australia's big four banks. The Port of Melbourne is the busiest shipping port in Australia, carrying 39 per cent of the country's exports. Melbourne's economic strength allowed it to weather the Global Financial Crisis (GFC), creating twice as many new jobs as Brisbane and Perth combined and welcoming more than a thousand new residents every week. Melbourne is booming, just as it has done before.

The city is not without its challenges. Though a major drought in the 1990s threatened the city's water supply, a pipeline to the Goulburn River and a desalination plant at Wonthaggi (to date unused) have secured its future. But it is how people move about the city that is proving to be one of the city's most critical issues. Pedestrian and cycle traffic continue to increase, but so too does road congestion, and the ageing public transport network groans.

In the 21st century, about a million people – residents, workers, students and tourists – visit the CBD every day. Beloved for its atmospheric laneways and opulent 19th century architecture, renowned for its coffee, bar, dining, shopping and sporting scenes, Melbourne is an upwardly mobile town. It's full of people that love to socialise and experience culture in whatever form it takes – whether at one of the many bookshops or literary events that make Melbourne a UNESCO City of Literature, or at a game of Aussie Rules, Test Cricket, Grand Slam Tennis, the Melbourne Cup or the Australian Grand Prix, all of which have helped make Melbourne the home of Australian sport. But that's only part of the story. You can be sure to find a festival of some kind on any given weekend, celebrating everything from film to fashion, steam trains to passata making, music and more. In Melbourne, you never know what you might find.

*PREVIOUS PAGES (left) Flinders Lane, circa 1910s, and cars have almost pushed out horses; (right) Amphlett Lane remembers Divinyls frontwoman Chrissie Amphlett. **BELOW** The 1888 Princes Bridge is the fourth bridge built on the site.*

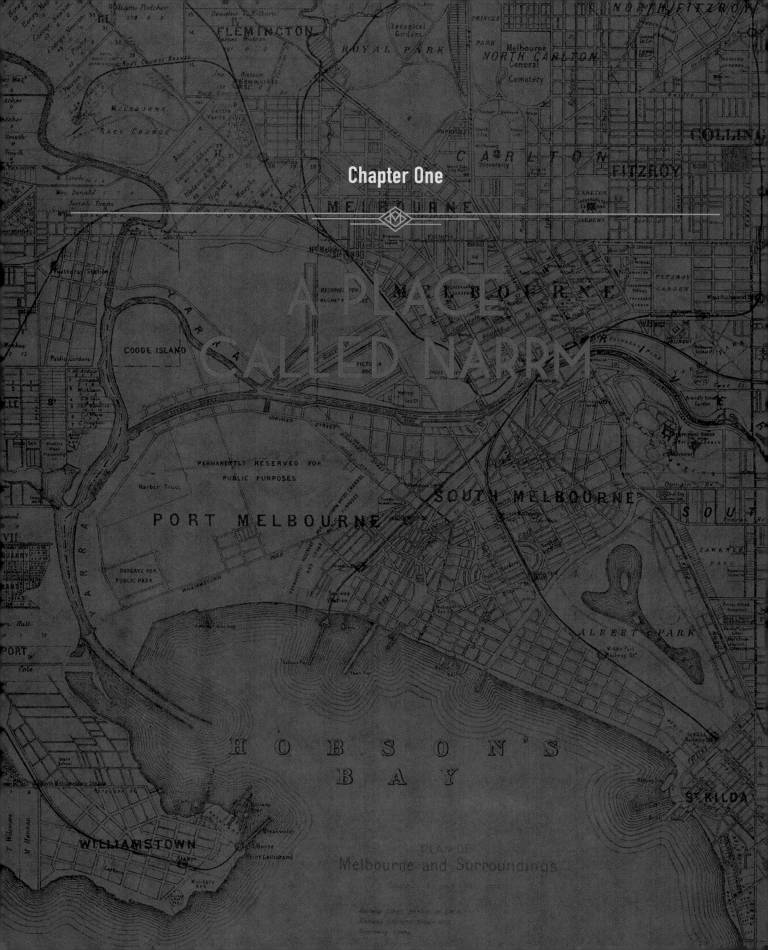

Chapter One

A PLACE
CALLED NARRM

The Kulin Nation

The history of the city of Melbourne is first the story of the dispossession of the Kulin Nation – an alliance of five distinct language groups: the Woi wurrung, Boon wurrung, Watha wurrung, Daung wurrung and Dja Dja wurrung peoples.

The patch of land on the Yarra River that early settler John Batman declared 'the place for a village' had for hundreds of generations been home to the peoples of the Kulin Nation. The soil was rich, the land flat for miles, encircled by the Macedon and Dandenong ranges – the work of volcanoes millions of years ago. Block faults created the large shallow depression we know as Port Phillip Bay.

The Woi wurrung, Boon wurrung and Watha wurrung met at campsites dotted throughout the area. They knew it as Narrm. They hunted for waterfowl in the rich swampland, cooked and ate shellfish along the coast, gathered ochre from the red cliffs at Point Ormond and quarried silcrete for stone tools on the Maribyrnong River. They forded the river at shallow waterfalls, like the one at Brimbank Park in Avondale Heights, later used by squatters to herd their sheep into the hinterland and back to town to market.

The people of the Kulin Nation worked about 30 hours a week fishing, hunting and gathering food in a balanced landscape abundant in waterfowl, tuber vegetables, small mammals and flowers. They made cloaks from possum skins, and decorated their linings with their histories, including the tale of the deity eagle Bunjil, who created all of the land, plants and people.

A 1971 archaeological dig at Keilor (*see* p. 184) uncovered a human hearth that has been radio-carbon-dated to about 31,000 years old, and a skull found at the site is believed to be up to 15,000 years old – during the last Ice Age when a land bridge still connected Tasmania with mainland Australia. Until about 10,000 years ago, the people of the Kulin Nation lived on the fertile plain of Port Phillip itself, now underwater.

Some 5000 years ago, the world began to heat up. Water levels rose even higher than they are now, covering south and west Melbourne, the shoreline extending along what is now St Kilda Rd, Spencer Street and out to Flemington. In time, the water receded again but all the while, the people of the Kulin Nation adapted; maintaining their intimate knowledge of the environment and sustaining their lifestyle within it.

Chapter Two

MELBOURNE CITY

The Yarra River

Melbourne's people and the Yarra River have an uneasy relationship. Sluggish, swollen, brown and murky, the Yarra has been dredged, diverted, blown up and polluted with industrial and human waste. But if it wasn't for the river we wouldn't be here. It is central to Melbourne's geography, and has determined how the city developed. Even today, we live either north or south of the river – still a subconscious expression of class.

The Yarra got its name from surveyor John Helder Wedge, who recorded the name 'Yarrow Yarrow' in his notebook on 13 September 1835, though as he later revealed he'd gotten it wrong: the Aboriginal people knew it as Birrarung; Yarra Yarra referred to the waterfall. The town was settled in its present location because of the fresh water beyond the falls. Aboriginal people had known this place a long time, hunting and gathering food around it for generations.

Surveyor Robert Hoddle noticed its usefully straight length, and aligned the city's grid (*see* p. 33) of streets to the Yarra. The city that was built virtually backed on to it, and it became a drain that conveniently swept away the detritus of life and industry. It was bridged over and used as a thoroughfare, but with few other water sources available until the reservoir at Yan Yean was opened in 1857, the Yarra River was also the place locals got their drinking water, washed their clothes and took a bath. The Upper Yarra Steam Gondola Co. ferried pleasure-seekers from the city to the Cremorne pleasure gardens (*see* p. 193) at Richmond in the 1850s and 1860s, the Henley-on-Yarra regattas attracted thousands well into the 20th century, and boathouses at Studley Park (*see* p. 196) and Fairfield are still popular recreation spots after more than 100 years, as is a barbie on the riverbank.

By the 20th century the worst of the abuse was over as the noxious trades relocated to Footscray and Flemington on the Maribyrnong River, and the underground sewerage system was finally completed in 1898. The Yarra, however, could give as good as it got. On Charles Grimes' 1803 survey, gardener James Flemming noted flood marks on trees six metres above ground level, and an 1863 flood stretched from the city all the way to Toorak Road. Sir John Coode's canal (*see* p. 93), built from 1886–92, mitigated flooding somewhat, and so too did late 19th century and early 20th century river widening, straightening and deepening schemes as far as Burnley in the city's south-east. The city's storm water systems have mostly prevented flooding since, but flash floods still occur. In 1934, 18 people were killed and

PREVIOUS PAGES (left) Elizabeth Street circa 1910, looking north-west from the Flinders Street Station clock tower; (right) the high-rise cityscape of today.

6000 left homeless as the Yarra turned into a giant lake from South Yarra to Warrandyte.

During the 1930s Melbourne town planners created parks along the river's edges, the Yarra Boulevard scenic drives in Richmond and Kew were built as an unemployment relief scheme, and parts of the Yarra and Maribyrnong riverbanks were lined with bluestone to prevent erosion. Finally the river was getting some love from the newcomers.

Freeways posed a new threat in the 1950s as planners looked to acquire the parks along the Yarra's banks. Few opposed the freeways passing through inner-suburban industrial areas, but there was outrage when they encroached on the sports fields of elite private schools in the eastern suburbs. With that came a renewed appreciation for the river. The Moomba Festival (*see* box) celebrated it from the 1950s, the *Herald* launched a 'Battle for the River' in the 1960s and the *Age* called on the government and the public to 'Give the Yarra a Go!' in the 1970s. By the 1980s more than 60 kilometres of the river was embraced by major parks at Yarra Bend, Warrandyte and the Yarra Valley.

New legislation, a planning scheme and public money saw the beginnings of a clean-up, but it was private finance that rejuvenated the Yarra in the central business district (CBD). Southbank (*see* p. 103) was first; more recently the focus has been at Docklands (*see* p. 87); Federation Square (*see* p. 67); and Fishermans Bend (*see* p. 84), all incorporating the river into the urban landscape, recasting the Yarra as picturesque. Even platypus have returned to the Yarra at Lilydale, and as close to the city as Merri Creek.

MOOMBA

CELEBRATING MELBOURNE and the Yarra River, the annual Moomba Festival attracts more than a million people to the city over the March Labour Day long weekend. When it started in 1955 the Anglican church called it 'hedonistic and embodying social decay'. There are fireworks displays, a major waterskiing competition, carnivals and parades led by prominent Melburnians, who are declared Moomba Monarchs. Certainly it's kitschy, but there's a special place in the hearts of Melburnians for the Birdman Rally, where competitors launch themselves from a bridge into the Yarra. The festival's irreverence is further encapsulated in the disputed etymology of the word Moomba, which is said to mean 'up your bum' in local Aboriginal languages.

The Hoddle Grid

Surveyor Robert Hoddle's CBD street grid, pegged out in 1837, has certainly proved to be visionary in terms of public utility. Hoddle marked out his grid's edges to align with the river and three small hills: the since decapitated Batman's Hill in the west, from where Hoddle made his observations (look out for the marker on the pedestrian overpass between Southern Cross Station and Etihad Stadium); Flagstaff Hill to the north; Bourke Hill in the east; and the Yarra to the south. And so a grid of broad streets carves up the city: one mile from Spencer Street at the bottom of Batman's Hill to Spring Street on Bourke Hill, half a mile across with Flinders Street neatly aligned to a straight stretch of the river.

The CBD was not Hoddle's only grid. Zoom out on a Google map and you'll spot the Hoddle Mile Grid – a separate grid at one mile spacing that extends into the city's hinterland, determining the orientation of roads and subdivisions across the suburbs from Cranbourne in the south-east to Werribee in the west. The chain that Hoddle used to mark out his survey is now in the collection of the State Library of Victoria (*see* p. 36), on display in the Changing Face of Victoria exhibition in the library's dome galleries.

The main streets were made broad not so much for their vistas as the need to accommodate bullock teams, and today they comfortably accommodate broad footpaths for pedestrians, trams, cars and even dedicated bike lanes. The little streets were added as service roads and from there, as blocks were divided and sold again, the city's famous laneway network grew; beloved today for being tucked away, off the beaten track or a shortcut from here to there.

STREET NAMES

A POPULAR children's mnemonic to remember the streets of Melbourne recounts the order of King, William, Queen and Elizabeth streets. Early Melbourne chronicler Garryowen tells us that King and William streets refer to the reigning monarch, William IV, and Queen for his consort Queen Adelaide. But Elizabeth? Hoddle is said to have named it for the Tudor Queen Elizabeth I, but it might also be for New South Wales' Governor Richard Bourke's wife, Elizabeth. Spencer, Russell and Spring streets were all named for British government officials of the day. Exhibition Street is named for the Exhibition Buildings, renamed in a vain attempt to escape the taint of the bawdy houses that operated in its vicinity. It was originally called Stephen Street, after another British government official.

The grid's central streets and the east–west streets are more local in flavour: Swanston Street for Charles Swanston, a founding member of John Batman's Port Phillip Association; Flinders Street for explorer Matthew Flinders, Collins Street for Lieutenant-Governor David Collins; Bourke Street for New South Wales' Governor Richard Bourke; Lonsdale Street for Melbourne's first police magistrate William Lonsdale, and La Trobe Street for the colony's first Lieutenant-Governor, Charles Joseph La Trobe.

Across the city, street names are products of their time. Victoria and Albert are the most common names, along with Park, Station and Railway. Many suburbs maintain their own unique nomenclatures, including Balaclava (Crimean War), Elwood (British writers), Ivanhoe (Heidelberg School artists) and Mitcham (Indian cities).

rebuilt in 1947 – making it one of the last picture palaces to be built in Australia. After it closed in 1970, its fittings and furnishings were auctioned in preparation for demolition to make way for Melbourne City Council's new City Square.

But things did not go to plan. In what was a decade of preservation wars, the Save the Regent Theatre Committee was formed and found an unlikely ally in the Builders Labourers Federation (BLF), whose leader Norm Gallagher remembered the Regent fondly, having worked there as a lolly boy.

Nevertheless, Lord Mayor Ron Walker (later chair of the Australian Grand Prix Corporation and developer of Crown Casino) pursued demolition, suggesting it wasn't worth preserving because it 'was not the Colosseum' and lamenting that the architects' vision for City Square would be limited if the Regent was to remain. By 1977, however, the Regent was saved. Premier Rupert Hamer recalled that he and his wife had courted there, declared the Regent a city landmark and legislated its protection.

City Square

By 1968 all the buildings on Swanston Street between Collins Street and Flinders Lane had been demolished to make way for the city's first square. Melbourne architects Denton Corker Marshall won the competition; their vision included a giant video screen, restaurants, cafes, shops, canopy, amphitheatre, graffiti wall, water wall and cascades, and an open area paved with sawn bluestone. The square also featured Melbourne's two most important sculptures: Charles Summers' 1865 Burke and Wills monument (*see* box, opposite) and Ron Robertson-Swann's specially commissioned Vault (*see* box).

When it was opened by Queen Elizabeth II in May 1980, City Square was immediately criticised for its starkness and the noise from the video screen. The location of the Burke and Wills monument was also noted – was it mockingly placed in the cascades? – as was its chlorine-damaged patina.

VAULT

RON ROBERTSON-SWANN'S large yellow geometric sculpture attracted the most scathing criticism of the City Square. Even before it had been built, the media, council and some sections of the public protested that the minimalist, postmodern artwork was unsympathetic to its intended location. And at $70,000 it didn't come cheap. The media dubbed it 'The Yellow Peril', though Robertson-Swann only named it *Vault* after it was installed in 1980. He knew it simply as 'The Thing'. The workers who assembled it called it 'Steelhenge' but whatever its name it was a headache for council. And so just six months after installing it the council banished it to Batman Park in the shadow of the railway viaduct on Flinders Street, where it remained for 20 years, covered in graffiti and oftentimes a shelter for the homeless. In 2002 it was relocated again to the grounds of the Australian Centre for Contemporary Art, where it has finally found its way into the hearts and on to the tea towels of Melburnians. In 2014, new tram barriers were installed along Swanston Street that in-the-know Melburnians will recognise riff off the *Vault* aesthetic.

Jacques Carabain's 1889 painting Melbourne Town Hall and Swanston Street, *which captures the new portico. The buildings in the background were demolished in the 1960s to make way for City Square; the one in the foreground is also gone.*

In the late 1990s, half the City Square was sold for the development of the Westin Hotel, and the remaining area simply made over with granite gravel and eucalypts. Though today it's more a forecourt than a public square, it was this redevelopment that facilitated the Regent Theatre, which had remained derelict for a quarter of a century, to be restored and eventually reopened for commercial musical theatre productions. As historian Graeme Davison has written, the Regent Theatre survives not because anyone said it was important but because trade unions and the public 'cherished the fake opulence and celluloid illusions of an old-time picture palace more than the magnificent emptiness of a city square'.

Melburnians had lived for almost 150 years without a public square. Built as a commercial town, Melbourne simply had no place for one. Though the public had agitated for a square since the 1840s, one never got up for fear of public demonstrations; as New South Wales Governor George Gipps put it, 'they only encourage democracy'. In October 2011, Lord Mayor Robert Doyle ordered an eviction of about 100 Occupy protestors from the City Square, which was reportedly enforced by as many as 400 riot police.

Melbourne Town Hall

At the corner of Collins and Swanston streets is the impressive bulk of the Melbourne Town Hall. The city's first town hall was begun in 1851 but work stalled with the onset of the gold rush and early Melburnians' lobbying for a bigger, better town hall. The foundation stone for today's town hall was laid in 1867 by the visiting Prince Alfred, Duke of Edinburgh. It was

MADAME BRUSSELS

PROMINENT IN Little Lon was Madame Brussels on Lonsdale Street in the second half of the 19th century. Though prostitution wasn't illegal, Madame Brussels achieved great notoriety in Marvellous Melbourne for the powerful and wealthy clientele she served – many of whom sat at Parliament just up the road. Other elite brothels nearby included Scotch Maude's, Biddy O'Connor's and Sarah Fraser's, where the visiting Prince Alfred was taken by the Commissioner of Police Captain Frederick Charles Standish during his 1867 tour of the colonies. Madame Brussels', however, was something else: a nondescript villa on the outside, inside it allegedly contained marble bathrooms,

opulent furnishings, carpets like meadow grass, nude sculptures and a private walled garden where patrons could enjoy champagne with the madame's 'girls'.

She audaciously listed her business in the first Melbourne telephone directory and once even paraded a young woman down Collins Street with a white feather in her hat, indicating her virginity could be had for a price. When the Victorian parliamentary mace was stolen in 1891, the story went that it had ended up in one of the brothels of Little Lon where it was used in a mock parliament. While there was never a parliamentary inquiry into its disappearance, the press conducted their own witch hunt. In the process, lord mayor and parliamentarian Samuel Gillott was revealed to have been an ongoing financier of Madame Brussels, and many politicians were discovered to have frequented her establishment. But as the madame said herself, if she talked 'divorce papers would fly thick and fast'.

Archaeological digs in 1988 and 2002 uncovered a wide variety of objects from abandoned cesspits, many of which are on display at the Melbourne Museum and in the foyer of 50 Lonsdale Street. These objects paint a picture of domestic life in 19th century Little Lon – a place where champagne flowed, women worked, and children played skittles and marbles in the streets.

BOURKE HILL

Just a block away from Little Lon and Chinatown, the top of Bourke Street is known as Bourke Hill, a popular restaurant destination. By the 1870s there were numerous restaurants as well as theatres, including Parer's Hotel and the Crystal Tea Rooms, as well as bohemian favourite Cafe de Paris. There were also pubs aplenty – of which only the Imperial remains – as well as oyster shops, billiard rooms, tobacconists and cigar divans, rifle galleries, bowling alleys and sideshows. At night the street was notorious for fighting and drunkenness. In its heyday there was more than a dozen theatres of every stripe in this precinct, and the city's largest market, at the corner of Bourke and Exhibition streets, was a sideshow unto itself. Today there are far fewer theatres than there used to be, but the Princess Theatre (*see* p. 49) on Spring Street remains the jewel in Melbourne's theatrical crown.

The Eastern Market started life as the rag-tag Paddy's Market in 1847 and grew to become the city's largest market, with fruit and vegetable merchants, sausage sellers, fortune tellers, and all manner of sideshow entertainers from dentists to phrenologists, jugglers to wrestlers, brass bands to trick dogs and the electro-shock therapist Madame Xena herself. Everyone from gold seekers to toffs, vagabonds to genteel families came here in search of fun, grinding their discarded oyster shells under foot. In the 1870s, architects Reed and Barnes won the contract to build a stately new market on the site (they'd recently completed the Melbourne Town Hall and were building the Exhibition Buildings at the time, and are still in business today as

The grand old Eastern Market, which stood at the corner of Bourke and Exhibition streets until 1960.

William Pitt's Princess Theatre is one among several landmark Victorian-era buildings on Spring Street.

Bates Smart), but its temporary closure saw business transferred to the Queen Victoria Market (*see* p. 70), never to return. Though the Eastern Market was described as commodious when it re-opened in 1879, with two-storeys, extensive cellars and even a fountain for merchants to wash their fruit and vegetables, most traders and their customers stayed at the Queen Victoria Market. The Eastern Market languished for decades – eventually demolished in 1960 to be replaced by the modern Southern Cross Hotel, host to visiting celebrities, Logie awards ceremonies and Liberal Party election soirees.

Princess Theatre

First built in 1854 by entrepreneur George Coppin and originally called Astley's Amphitheatre, the theatre featured a central ring for equestrian, as well as a stage for performance. It was renamed Princess Theatre in 1857 after a renovation, and rebuilt entirely in 1885 when William Pitt (*see* box, p. 46) was commissioned to build the current theatre, which when completed featured marble staircases and the world's first retractable roof.

A testament to Melbourne's wealth, Hotel Windsor predates other more famous grand hotels including Singapore's Raffles (1887), London's Savoy (1889), New York's The Plaza and the Waldorf Astoria (both 1894) and Paris's Hotel Ritz (1898).

While performing as Mephistopheles in the opera *Faust* on 3 March 1888, singer Frederick Federici had a heart attack and died just as his character disappeared dramatically through a trapdoor in the floor. Though he never came back on stage, his fellow actors insisted he had taken his bows with them, and the story of his ghost has haunted the theatre ever since.

In 1933 the theatre was purchased by the theatre entrepreneur F.W. Thring. He had his initials carved over the proscenium arch after he made the theatre home of his radio station 3XY, which began broadcasting in 1935. By the 1970s it was the number one radio station in Melbourne though its popularity soon declined with the advent of FM radio. 3XY is now Magic 1278. After the closure of the radio station in the 1980s, new theatre entrepreneur David Marriner bought the Princess Theatre in 1987, renovated, and reopened it in 1989.

Hotel Windsor

This Second Empire masterpiece is the last of Australia's grand 19th century hotels. Built in 1883 as the Grand Hotel, it was expanded and converted to a coffee palace in 1886 by temperance advocate and land boomer James Munro, who famously burnt the hotel's liquor licence in the street. Munro was bankrupted during the depression of the 1890s and a new owner further expanded the hotel in 1897 to take in the White Hart Hotel on the corner of Bourke and Spring streets. The Australian Constitution was drafted here in 1898, and celebrities, sporting heroes and royalty have all stayed here. By the 1970s, however, the Duchess of Spring Street was decidedly out of favour, and the city lost its other great 19th century hotels: the Menzies and the Federal. The Windsor is now recognised as being nationally significant, and today it's famous for its high teas and old-time Cricketers' Bar. But with adjacent apartment towers pushing ever skyward there are new arguments about overshadowing and airspace.

Italians of Bourke Hill

In the 20th century, Bourke Hill attracted Italian restaurateurs. Before Benito Mussolini became prime minister of Italy in 1922, there were fewer than 8000 Italians living in Victoria but by 1930 there were 25,000 who had come to escape fascism. At first they put their vineyard and market gardening skills to good use across the state, but in 1928 newly arrived Rinaldo Massoni purchased Samual Wynn's Cafe Denat on Bourke Street, changed its name to Cafe Florentino and transformed it into an Italian restaurant. (Wynn went on to establish himself as a winemaker at Coonawarra in South Australia, and his label survives today.) Florentino became Grossi Florentino in 1999 when celebrity chef Guy Grossi bought the business. Guiseppe Codognotto opened the Italian Workers Club (later Society) in 1932. Down the road, Pellegrini's claim to have brought the first espresso machine to Melbourne in 1954, though that remains hotly contested. Either way, the restaurant is a local icon — famous for more than half a century for its cursive neon sign, Italian-speaking waiters, red vinyl stools and family favourites such as cheesy lasagne. In nearby Meyers Place, the Waiters Club is a late-night institution for hospitality workers come to unwind over a carafe and homestyle pasta at formica tables.

The iconic Pellegrini's neon sign.

CHINATOWN

Along Little Bourke Street between the bright red Paifang on Swanston Street and the Tianjin Gardens – which commemorate Melbourne's Chinese sister city – on Spring Street, Chinatown is the world's second-oldest continuous Chinese settlement outside China. Established in 1851 with the onset of the Victorian gold rush, tens of thousands of Chinese passed through here en route to the goldfields. Indeed, by the 1860s Chinese accounted for 20 per cent of the men on the diggings. Unlike their European counterparts, who toiled at their own expense in the hope they'd strike it rich, Chinese diggers were paid fixed wages by Chinese entrepreneurs.

From the beginning of the gold rush, the Chinese established a supply chain from the diggings all the way to China. Their enclave on Little Bourke Street was the halfway point – a convenient location for lodging houses and merchant businesses supplying tools for the job ahead. As early as the 1850s, there were numerous opium dens, too. Celestial Avenue off Little Bourke was named for them.

Melbourne's Chinatown has always maintained an entrepreneurial quality. They've had to: government policy was plainly discriminatory – including residential taxes and culminating in the *Immigration Restriction Act* 1901, otherwise known as the White Australia Policy.

When the gold rush began to wane, Chinese diggers moved to Melbourne, congregating around Little Bourke Street. They turned their attention to furniture making, establishing grocery stores and laundries and of course restaurants.

By the 1930s, Chinatown was popular with university students for cheap meals, and by the 1970s had become popularised to such an extent that Chinatown was officially designated a tourist and heritage precinct by the Melbourne City Council and state government. That decade also saw the repeal of the White Australia Policy by the progressive Whitlam government – at last ending state-sanctioned racial discrimination and precipitating increased immigration from Singapore, Malaysia, Taiwan, Hong Kong and China.

The opening of the Museum of Chinese Australian History in 1985 as well as the increasingly popular Chinese New Year celebrations gave the precinct a cultural focus. The Dr Sun Yat-sen memorial in the museum's forecourt commemorates the centenary of the

OPPOSITE Chinatown is ablaze with colour at night.

Buskers outside the GPO with Simon Perry's Public Purse *at left.*

A PUBLIC CONVENIENCE

ON HEFFERNAN Lane, you'll find a hand-painted sign that reads 'Commit No Nuisance'. This is a relic of Marvellous Smellbourne, the city's sobriquet before that most marvellous of inventions: a sewerage system. Until the late 1890s, Melbourne's lanes provided coverage for quick relief. South Melbourne-made cast-iron urinals were provided at street corners from as early as 1859, though women didn't get their own public convenience until 1902, when underground toilets were opened at the corner of Bourke and Russell streets (they're now sealed under a public artwork). The oldest functioning public toilet in the city is at the corner of Queen and Collins streets.

founding of the Republic of China, and the Chinese New Year Lion Dance ends with a blessing of the statue. The museum's extensive collection of Chinese clothing and textiles, photographs, documents and artefacts reflects Chinese community life in Australia since the 1850s. Its centrepiece is the 2003 Dai Loong – the Millennium Dragon – the largest Chinese dragon in the world.

Chinatown also sports fierce culinary credentials. The Flower Drum on Market Lane is considered among the world's best imperial Chinese restaurants, and the Hutong Dumpling Bar across the lane is one of the city's most popular restaurants with regular queues for their famous xiao long bao. The humble Australian dim sim – readily available from fish and chip shops around the country – is widely believed to have been invented in Chinatown in 1945, though unsurprisingly its provenance remains disputed. A lobby group has formed to build a monument commemorating the dimmie; we can only hope it features a fountain of soy sauce.

Unlike City Square, Federation Square was hatched by the Victorian state government. It replaced the 1960s Gas and Fuel Corporation which many regarded as an eyesore. Redevelopment of the area also meant the diversion of Batman Avenue – and the Route 70 tram – which once skirted the north bank of the river to terminate at St Kilda Road.

Designed by LAB Architecture, Federation Square is a U-shape of buildings around a main square. The subterranean 'Labyrinth', located above old railway platforms and below the main square, is a concrete honeycomb passive cooling system that moderates the temperature in the square's glass atrium, using just one-tenth of the energy of conventional air conditioning.

Inside you'll find the Melbourne Visitor Centre, National Gallery of Victoria's Ian Potter Centre and the Australian Centre for the Moving Image. The auditorium, overlooking the river, is a popular venue for Melbourne International Arts Festival and Melbourne Writers Festival events.

Traditional Melbourne bluestone links the Atrium and St Paul's Court with the rest of the city's footpaths, but it's the square's staggering 470,000 ochre-coloured sandstone blocks from Western Australia that steal the show.

In 2006 the Federation Wharf precinct opened, extending Federation Square to the Yarra by redeveloping the vaults in the shadow of the Princes Bridge with cafes and refurbished ferry terminals. A further expansion to cover the remaining area of railyards to the east of the main square is still regularly dreamed about.

ABOVE Deborah Halpern's Angel, initially installed in the moat out front of the National Gallery on St Kilda Road, now located on Birrarung Marr beside the Yarra River. OPPOSITE Federation Square, still controversial into its second decade.

SPEAKERS CORNER

THE 20-ACRE Birrarung Marr – river of mists in the local Woi wurrung language – has uninterrupted sight lines for viewing some of Melbourne's icons, and it contains a few treasures of its own. At its eastern extent you'll find a series of mounds ringed in bluestone. This area was once known as Speakers Corners, a location for public lectures and protests – most notably the anti-conscription rallies of 1916. In lieu of a city square Melburnians had to come up with their own solution for mass gatherings, and down by the river emerged as a happy compromise for the citizens and the local council. Since the advent of mass literacy, television and other forms of entertainment, interest in public speaking has waned, though every Sunday you'll still encounter someone with a microphone, an amp and some well-thumbed notes on the steps of the State Library (*see* p. 36).

Queen Victoria Market, 1907.
***BELOW** Located at the top end of
I Shed, the American Doughnut
Kitchen has been an institution for
locals and visitors seeking a sweet fix
since the 1950s.*

QUEEN VICTORIA MARKET

The Queen Victoria Market on Victoria Street is the city's leading market. Along with
the Prahran and South Melbourne markets, the Queen Victoria Market is a rare surviving
Victorian-era market. It is the largest and oldest open-air market in the Southern Hemisphere,
but it was not Melbourne's first market. It was preceded by the Western Market (built in 1841
on the block bounded by Market, Collins and William streets and Flinders Lane) and the larger
Eastern Market (*see* p. 48).

The Queen Victoria Market was established in 1857 due to overcrowding at the Eastern
Market. It had not been initially popular, so was used as a livestock and hay market until 1867,
then a meat and fish market. New sheds were added in 1878 and the Queen Victoria Market
became the city's main – though it was meant to only be temporary – wholesale and retail fruit
and vegetable market.

The Elizabeth Street shops were added in 1880 and the Meat and Fish Hall facade
constructed in 1884. As the market grew over the next 50 years, its operators looked next door
to expand into the old cemetery. About a thousand bodies were re-interred to make way for the
market's expansion – my mother's great-great aunt among them – but it is believed that more

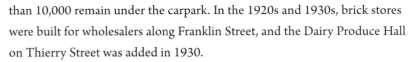

than 10,000 remain under the carpark. In the 1920s and 1930s, brick stores
were built for wholesalers along Franklin Street, and the Dairy Produce Hall
on Thierry Street was added in 1930.

The postwar population boom, however, soon led to market
overcrowding. Corruption, extortion and racketeering were exposed during
the early 1960s Market Wars, leading to the murders of several market
stall holders. The relocation of the wholesale market to new premises in
West Melbourne in 1969, however, did not resolve the market's challenges.

Chapter Three

PORT

PORT MELBOURNE
FISHERMANS BEND
DOCKLANDS
WEST MELBOURNE

MELBOURNE'S PORT FACILITIES, historic and new, are spread

across a vast area of inner Melbourne. From 1835 vessels moored at the riverbank out the front of Customs House on Flinders Street and later to stakes driven into the river. But the little river – narrow, shallow, winding and full of snags – was never going to be a permanent home to the city's port activities. That role fell also to Williamstown (see p. 165) and Sandridge (later Port Melbourne, see p. 82) before the lower reaches of the Yarra were transformed by Sir John Coode (see p. 93), his canal and the largest dock in the world.

Over the years shipping channels through Port Phillip have been blasted, widened and dredged to serve Australia's largest and busiest cargo port, handling almost 40 per cent of the nation's container traffic. But with the port already at full capacity and ships getting bigger and bigger still, shipping may yet be pushed out of Port Phillip altogether.

First wharves

In what was perhaps Melbourne's first public-private partnership, the entrepreneurial Captain George Cole built Melbourne's first wharf on Flinders Street, between King and Spencer streets, in 1841. By the end of the decade Coles Wharf had storage sheds, a bonded warehouse and accommodation for the customs officer.

Convicts built a stone jetty at Williamstown in 1839, but the captains of large ships were forced to anchor in the bay, off Sandridge, owing to the sandbar at the river's mouth. There, they waited for Wilbraham Liardet (see box, p. 83) to pick them up in his whaleboat. Whether you landed in Williamstown or off Sandridge, you still faced an uncomfortable and expensive journey to town by horse or bullock dray. Or you walked.

Following Separation in 1851 (see p. 22), the new Victorian government took control of the port. Williamstown was devoted to ship building, particularly for the new military. In 1853 the government doubled the city wharves, providing more than 1000 metres of wharf from Queens Bridge to well beyond Spencer Street. The south bank of the river was leased for shipping and associated services from the 1850s, and a pier opened at Sandridge in 1854 – and with it the first railway in Australia (see p. 82) connecting the port to the city.

An 1860 royal commission into the management of Melbourne's port facilities finally led to the establishment of a port authority. At this time there were wharves for 36 vessels on the Yarra in town, compared with 43 each at Williamstown and Sandridge.

In 1877 the Melbourne Harbour Trust was established. Following a major flood in 1878, Melbourne's port was redefined. A canal was dug to shorten the river by almost three kilometres (completed 1886) and Victoria Dock (*see* p. 91), the largest dock in the world, was begun in 1892. Appleton Dock was begun in 1913 (completed 1956), and a central pier was added to Victoria Dock in 1916. Now it's encircled by apartment and office towers, one designed to look like the prow of a ship.

At Port Melbourne, Princes Pier was built in 1912 (*see* p. 82) and Railway Pier was replaced and renamed Station Pier in 1930 (*see* p. 82).

Shipping upstream of Spencer Street was cut off in 1927 with the opening of the Batman Bridge, and again by the Charles Grimes Bridge in 1975 and the Bolte Bridge (*see* p. 89) in 1998. Containers were first berthed at Swanson Dock in 1969, and along with Webb and Appleton docks now handle the majority of Melbourne's shipping cargo.

*ABOVE A forest of pylons hint at the extent of Princes Pier. **PREVIOUS PAGES** (left) Photographer Charles Nettleton captured the activity of Railway Pier under its forest of masts in the 1860s; (right) The design of the pedestrian-only Webb Bridge references an Aboriginal fishing trap.*

PORT MELBOURNE

An industrial and increasingly fashionable 'middle-class' neighbourhood, Port Melbourne has experienced massive population growth in the last two decades; its beaches and proximity to the city ensuring its gentrification.

First called Sandridge for the sandbar off shore, Port Melbourne's European history formally began in 1839 with the arrival of Wilbraham Frederick Evelyn Liardet (*see* box, p. 83), who built the first jetty and established postal and ferry services to Melbourne. For most of the 19th and 20th centuries Port Melbourne's piers were the gateway to Melbourne for hundreds of thousands of immigrants. There are fewer passenger ships these days – about 70 cruise ships a year and the daily *Spirit of Tasmania* ferry.

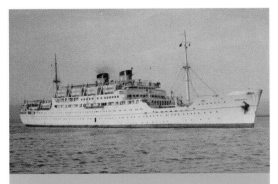

SURRIENTO

MY FATHER'S family came to Australia from Italy in the 1950s. My nonno sailed for Australia aboard the *Surriento* (above) in 1951, followed two years later by my uncles aged 15 and 16. My nonna brought the youngest children out in 1955 – reuniting her family after five years, on the farm that my nonno and uncles had begun clearing at Nerrena in South Gippsland. This story is not an uncommon one among migrant families. Indeed, by the 1970s, the main reason given for migration was family reunion.

Station Pier and Australia's First Railway

After the first land sales in the area in 1850, Sandridge's role as a port continued to grow. Realising that transport could be more easily and cheaply conveyed by rail rather than river, a pier was built at Port Melbourne and with it Australia's first railway, which opened on 12 September 1854. Surveyor Robert Hoddle had suggested the railway in 1838, nominating the route still more or less in use today as the 109 light rail. Even today, cruise ship passengers can retrace the steps of gold rush immigrants from the port to the city.

Despite acting as the landing spot for prospective miners and settlers, Sandridge was relatively neglected during the gold-rush years. From 1860 to 1890 Port Melbourne took on a distinctive working-class character as the port grew to accommodate increasing amounts of passengers and cargo. A second pier, Princes Pier, was built by the Melbourne Harbour Trust in 1912.

By the 1920s, however, Railway Pier – the longest timber piled wharf in Australia – could no longer accommodate the new large steamships, so Station Pier was built to replace it. Opening in 1930, it was almost a kilometre in length and capable of berthing ships over 300 metres long. The timber supports of the old pier are still underneath, chopped down in the name of progress. The two-storey terminals cleverly received cargo at pier level, passengers above.

From the 1850s until the 1960s Port Melbourne was the entry to Melbourne for hundreds of thousands of migrants. First came the gold seekers, then the assisted migrants, mostly from England, Ireland and Germany. By the end of World War II, the Curtin and Chifley governments' mantra was 'Populate or Perish', even if it did dilute the White Australia Policy (*see* p. 53). The term 'Ten Pound Poms' refers to British adults who paid £10 for their passage; their children travelled free. The government's assisted migration scheme was gradually extended to other European nations – first to the whitest northern Europeans, later to southern Europeans and then all refugees from the war.

With the advent of containerisation and international air travel in the 1960s, use of Station and Princes piers declined. Princes Pier in particular fell into disrepair and several stores were destroyed by fire in the 1990s and 2000s. In the 2010s it was partly restored and its seaward end removed, leaving a forest of piles to suggest the pier's history.

Port Melburnians, so long a working class people, provided labour for less-skilled and often lower-paid occupations in the manufacturing, shipping and transport industries. During the 1930s Depression, unemployment – tenanted mainly by wharf labourers – was estimated to be as high as 80 per cent.

WILBRAHAM LIARDET

ACCORDING TO William Westgarth in his recollections of early Melbourne, Wilbraham Frederick Evelyn Liardet was a character: 'A kind of roving Garibaldi, minus indeed, the hero's war-paint and the Italian unity, but with all his frankness and indomitable resource'. Liardet arrived in Melbourne in 1839 with his wife and nine children. They were en route to Sydney, but decided to settle here instead. Liardet and his young sons secured the boating of 'the Beach' (featured above in painting), so that sometimes Sandridge was even called 'Liardet's Beach'. Liardet bought a whaleboat and carried mail ashore from ships, and by August 1840 was running a mail cart into town three times a day. In October he opened a hotel and began a passenger service through the scrub to Melbourne. He also built the first jetty.

As the town prospered, so too did the Liardets. Wilbraham enjoyed fishing and entertaining the community by playing the guitar and flute, as well as singing, and organising sports such as regattas, horse racing and archery. He is perhaps best remembered for his primitive watercolours, some of the earliest likenesses made of Melbourne.

Liardet and his family, however, weren't the first Europeans to establish themselves at Port Melbourne. They were two beachcombers from Van Diemen's Land (Tasmania) known as Davis and Storey, who allegedly lived in an old sugar barrel, just like Huckleberry Finn, fishing and smuggling to get by.

SWALLOW AND ARIELL BISCUIT FACTORY

THE SMELL of fresh-baked biscuits must have been welcome, though perhaps unexpected, for immigrants disembarking at Port Melbourne after a 100-day sea journey. Founded in 1854, Swallow and Ariell was once Australia's number one biscuit company. By the 1880s, their Port Melbourne factory covered almost the entire block bounded by Stoke, Rouse, Princes and Beach streets; they owned flour mills and sugar plantations in the Goulburn Valley and Queensland; and the company was reputed to be the fifth-largest biscuit company in the world. In their early days they manufactured ship biscuits, meat biscuits (apparently taken by Burke and Wills on their expedition, *see* p. 40) as well as cakes and puddings. Best remembered for their Uneeda and Teddy Bear biscuits, Swallow and Ariell was absorbed first by the Australian Biscuit Co. in 1964 and later by Arnott's. Parts of the factory still stand, now occupied by apartments.

FISHERMANS BEND AND SOUTH WHARF

From the 1850s, the lower reaches of the Yarra, known as 'Humbug Reach' and 'Fishermen's Bend' were occupied by under-employed fishermen. Some 30 families lived on 'the Bend', accepting dockside work when it was available, otherwise living off the land, fishing in the bay, collecting water from sail canvases and sleeping in rough shacks made from timber, corrugated iron and flattened kerosene tins. The last of the shacks was demolished in 1970 to make way for Webb Dock, but descendants of the Bend fishermen still cast out in the bay.

Today, Fishermans Bend is a key industrial hub – home to Holden, Kraft, the *Herald & Weekly Times* printery, aeronautical and maritime research laboratories as well as Westgate Park, a rehabilitated wetland habitat in the shadow of the Westgate Bridge – but its future is part of the Victorian government's urban renewal strategy. Draft visions include creating 40,000 jobs and housing up to 80,000 new residents in medium and high density accommodation, serviced by new train and tram links, by 2050.

Commonwealth Aircraft Corporation

It was at Fishermans Bend that Australian modern aviation manufacturing was developed. After Essington Lewis, the general manager of BHP, returned from a 1935 visit to Europe, he was convinced that war was inevitable and concerned about Australia's lack of capacity in the industry. The Commonwealth Aircraft Corporation was formed by a collaboration of major Australian companies – among them BHP, General Motors Holden, the Imperial Chemical Industries of Australia and New Zealand Co., the Orient and Steam Navigation Company, Electrolytic Zinc and the Broken Hill Associated Smelter. Most of these companies were associated with the powerful Collins House syndicate. Managed by Lawrence Wackett, the company's first

A major flood in the late 1870s was the catalyst for the next development proposal. Engineer John Coode (*see* p. 93) was commissioned to widen and reroute the Yarra and excavate three new docks: Victoria, Appleton and Swanson. Coode Island was created in the process, though the original course of the Yarra has long since been filled in. Flinders Street was also extended to link the wharves and a wall built to retain what was left of Batman's Hill.

By the mid 1980s, containerisation of shipping saw rail and sea freight facilities move out of Victoria Dock and concentrated at Appleton, Swanson and Webb docks. The rave scene moved in, the club kids partying in the enormous sheds far from the eyes and ears of the rest of Melbourne. In 1991, the Docklands Authority was formed to co-ordinate revitalisation of the site. It has been no easy task, but a new waterfront precinct has emerged with offices and apartment towers and the 52,000 seat Etihad Stadium catering to hundreds of thousands of office workers, residents and tourists every year.

Bolte Bridge

Spanning the Yarra, Denton Corker Marshall's late 1990s Bolte Bridge with its decorative pylons forms part of the CityLink tollway and connects the Tullamarine Freeway to the airport with the

Bolte Bridge links the Westgate and Tullamarine freeways while guarding the entrance to Victoria Harbour.
OPPOSITE *Proposed design for the extension of the city westward, showing an ornamental lakes in the shape of England and Ireland.*

NO. 2 GOODS SHED

CONSTRUCTED IN 1889 and originally called A Goods Shed, it was the longest single building in Australia at the time. The 370 metre shed was made from polychromatic Hawthorn bricks with bluestone sills, its slate tiled gable roof supported by cast-iron columns. There are 26 arched doors on the east side and 28 on the west side. There were loading platforms for horse-drawn vehicles on the outside, and rail platforms to three tracks internally.

As part of the redevelopment of Docklands, the shed was cut in half by the extension of Collins Street right through the centre of it. Both sections have now been refurbished.

ABOVE The No. 2 Goods Shed is today a rare piece of heritage architecture among the glass and steel towers of 21st century Docklands. *BACKGROUND* The grand opening of the No. 2 Goods Shed.

Westgate Freeway. It is named for Sir Henry Bolte, Victoria's longest-serving premier (1955–72) and commissioner of the Tullamarine, Westgate and Monash freeways, Melbourne's first international airport at Tullamarine and two universities (Monash and La Trobe).

Bolte was also an ardent supporter of capital punishment as a deterrent to violent crime. After Ronald Ryan (*see* p. 157) was convicted of murdering a prison guard during an escape from Pentridge Prison (*see* p. 156), Bolte ignored all calls for clemency and determined that Ryan's death sentence be upheld. Ryan's hanging in February 1967 alienated the press, religious leaders, academics, most of the legal profession and even sections of the Liberal Party, but Bolte was re-elected that year with an increased majority. As Henry Bolte later relayed to Jeff Kennett, 'If you want to get (elected), you'll introduce capital punishment.'

Victoria Dock

Victoria Dock is the oldest and largest surviving single dock in the world. It was built to accommodate ships of 9.5 metre draft, with initially timber wharf sheds and wharves around the perimeter, supplemented by a piled timber central pier in 1919 extending from the east edge of the dock. The Central Pier retains two sheds but has been reduced to half its size. It is so big that in 1925 it hosted 26 vessels from the visiting American navy. The Central Pier retains two sheds but has been reduced to half its size.

Surrounding the dock today, now renamed Victoria Harbour, are numerous office and apartment towers, retail spaces and hotels. In the Stadium Precinct is a digital broadcasting centre, while Waterfront City is a shopping and entertainment area that includes the now-operational Melbourne Star Observation Wheel, and bronze statues of Melbourne entertainment icons including Kylie Minogue, John Farnham, Graham Kennedy, Dame Nellie Melba and Dame Edna. There is also a film and television studio with five sound stages.

Southern Cross Station

The main terminus for interstate and Victorian country rail and bus services, Southern Cross Station has been a major transport terminus ever since La Trobe granted 50 acres to the Melbourne, Mount Alexander & Murray Railway Co. to build a line to Echuca in 1852. When the Victorian Government took over that project in 1858 Spencer Street Station, as it was known until the 2000s, became the focus of the Victorian Railways.

Southern Cross Station under construction in 2005.

The site was Batman's Hill, the location of John Batman's first house built in 1835. Both the house and the hill were removed to make way for the station. A plaque on the Wailing Wall commemorates the location of John Batman's House.

By the 1860s, there was a platform and goods sheds, and new passenger platforms were added in the 1870s. In 1891, Spencer Street Station was connected to Flinders Street by a viaduct, and the station was enlarged again in 1924 with additional passenger platforms. The station was reconstructed in 1962 to accommodate the standardisation of railway gauges across the country (until then, each state's train tracks were different widths, requiring passengers to change trains at state borders). Subways connected the platforms, and a giant mural was commissioned to celebrate transport throughout the ages. Since the station was redeveloped as Southern Cross in 2006 that mural has almost disappeared behind shop walls but at least the station now links the city with Docklands (*see* p. 87), rather than acting as the barrier between them. The enormous and distinctive undulating roof by Grimshaw architects helps vent fumes from the station.

The Wailing Wall

In 1890 Flinders Street became the first of the Hoddle Grid streets to be extended west. A polychromatic Hawthorn brick wall stretched its length from the Flinders Street Viaduct to the No. 2 Goods Shed, with the extension improving access to the wharves and rail yards, and the wall retaining the last vestiges of Batman's Hill.

Though the last of Batman's Hill was removed in 1892, the wall gained new importance as a site where wharf labourers gathered. Until the 1940s, stevedores employed wharfies using the bull system of labour hire. Workers assembled twice daily at the stevedores' offices on the south side of Flinders Street and were picked from a line-up based on their physical condition and attitude. Those who missed out were forbidden from loitering out front –sometimes being moved on by police – and so they soon began to congregate on the opposite side of the street.

1988 AUSTRALIAN WATERFRONT DISPUTE

THE APPLETON and Swanson Docks were the site of the 1998 Australian Waterfront Dispute, a watershed event in Australian industrial relations history. The dispute arose when stevedoring giant Patrick Corporation restructured its operations without tellings its workers.

Australian waterfront productivity had been the subject of business and government inquiries since the 1980s. A 1997 productivity commission found that shipping through Australian ports was more expensive but slower and less reliable than overseas. This resulted in the highest costs to shippers. Patrick Corporation sought to improve productivity by offering redundancies, reducing overtime entitlements and casualising its workforce.

Prime Minister John Howard's federal government was concurrently busy introducing Australian workplace agreements, which sought to foster individual choice in workplace bargaining and simultaneously reduce the power of unions, particularly to undertake collective bargaining. On the waterfront, however, this was an idea only ever toyed with due to the opposition from the powerful Maritime Union.

In September 1997, Patrick Corporation divided business operations into two companies: one that owned its stevedoring business, another that employed its workforce. The stevedoring business entered into new labour supply agreements with the workforce business but no one told the union – on purpose because the new labour supply agreements were terminable in the event of industrial action. After Patrick's employees went on strike in late 1997 and early 1998, Patrick's dismissed its entire workforce, liquidated its assets, and imposed a lockout at its wharves. By the following morning, Patrick's docks were fully operational with non-union staff.

Though the Howard government supported Patrick in their action, the Federal Court and later the full bench of the High Court found that Patrick had deliberately restructured the company to dismiss its unionised workers. By June 1998, the company and the Maritime Union had negotiated a new work agreement in which the permanent workforce was nearly halved through voluntary redundancy, casualisation and contracting out. The company took control of rostering, while the union retained the ability to represent its members. The non-union workers who had been employed to break the union were sacked at the conclusion of the dispute.

SIR JOHN MONASH

GENERAL SIR John Monash, was born in West Melbourne on 27 June 1865. His Jewish parents' high expectations were met when he graduated dux of the school at Scotch College, attended the University of Melbourne and studied in his own time at the Public Library. He dropped out of university when his mother got sick, finding work as an engineer on the construction of Princes Bridge, and eventually graduated in 1887. In 1888, he was entrusted to lead the construction of the Outer Circle Railway line (*see* p. 199).

He maintained an interest in the military corps from the mid 1880s, and in 1913 was made a colonel. His 4th Brigade landed at Gallipoli on 26 April 1915. That was a disastrous campaign but the brigade had performed admirably, and by July Monash had been made a brigadier-general – despite the rumours that he was a German spy. After the evacuation from Gallipoli in December he and his brigade went on to defend the Suez Canal and then to France, where he was strategically involved in several campaigns so successful they turned the war — and Monash was knighted by King George V on 12 August 1918. Perhaps his greater achievement was the repatriation of 160,000 Australian troops in just eight months after the armistice.

Following his return from war he became the general manager of the State Electricity Commission of Victoria, overseeing the development of the Yallourn power station in the La Trobe Valley, and was the driving force behind the construction of the Shrine of Remembrance (*see* p. 109). He died in 1931 and is remembered in Monash University and the Monash Freeway.

Flagstaff Gardens is today popular with nearby office workers for rest and recreation. **OPPOSITE** *A Canberra bomber, built onsite, taxis into the Commonwealth Aircraft Corporation hanger at Fishermans Bend, circa 1940s.*

Flagstaff Gardens

Melbourne's oldest public gardens were laid out in the early 1860s on Flagstaff Hill – where a flagstaff had been erected in 1840 to convey messages between town and ships in the bay. Before that, the hill had been the city's first cemetery, relocated to the site of the Queen Victoria Market (*see* p. 70). A sandstone obelisk erected in 1871 commemorates the first interments. In 1850 the gardens were the scene of celebration when news of Separation (*see* p. 22) reached Melbourne, but its attraction as a place of rendezvous diminished with the coming of the electric telegraph. The signal station briefly became an observatory, though it too was soon superseded by the Melbourne Observatory (*see* p. 121). Promenaders from those days would not recognise the gardens today. Office towers entirely obscure the views of the bay and Williamstown, the knock-off classical statues are long gone, and lawns and flower beds have replaced mass plantings of trees.

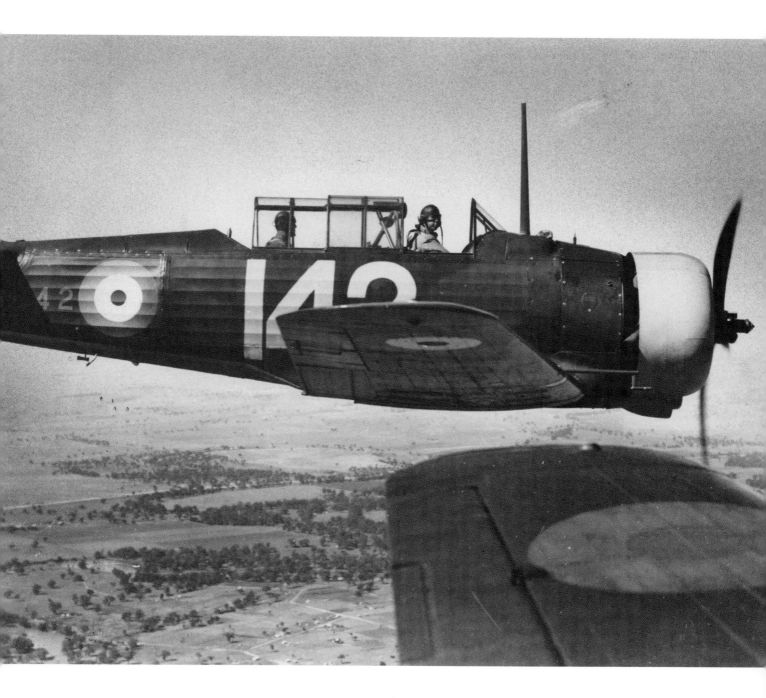

NORTH

MELBOURNE'S NORTH HAS a rich and varied story. It's home to the state's oldest university, the city's first suburb and the brickyards of Victoria. Warehouses and factories once occupied almost entire suburbs and provided employment for workers in tiny terrace houses. From the Old Melbourne Gaol to HM *Pentridge* Prison, Melbourne's north also contains a multitude of fascinating true crime stories. These days, though, you're more likely to see baristas on bicycles as gentrification has taken place and the area's economy is the strongest it has ever been. Its major north–south roads Sydney Road, Lygon Street and High Street are flourishing; new apartment developments have brought increased density; and bars, cafes and boutiques have brought tertiary-educated, socially, environmentally and culturally aware Melburnians together in the city's north.

Before bricks and mortar

ABOVE *Florence Ada Fuller's 1885 portrait of Wurundjeri elder and artist William Barak.* **PREVIOUS PAGES** *(left) Carlton & United Breweries workers in 1938. New developments on the old brewery site; (right) Modern architecture.*

The northern suburbs' bluestone quarries all harvest basalt created from volcanic activity millions of years ago. An enormous eruption at Mount Fraser near Beveridge filled the ancient valleys of the Merri and Darebin creeks with molten rock, reaching as far south as the Yarra River at Richmond. Until the arrival of squatter John Batman and friends in the 1830s, the area was covered by grassy open woodlands dominated by River Red Gums and Yellow Box, and favoured by kangaroos and wallabies. The ground was occasionally swampy around what is now Coburg and Brunswick, where there were also rich clay deposits.

Aboriginal people moved with the seasons throughout the area, hunting for game and foraging as they went. At Mt William, near present-day Lancefield, they quarried stone to grind seed and make tools and weapons, all of which were traded extensively across south-eastern Australia. Though its exact location may never be known, Batman's 'treaty' is said to have taken place in the city's north – perhaps on the banks of the Merri or Darebin creeks or even the Plenty River. The confluence of the Yarra River and Merri Creek was also a meeting point for generations. While Indigenous people were pushed out of most of the rest of Melbourne, they created communities in Brunswick and particularly around Gertrude and Smith streets in Fitzroy, where today they are more visible than anywhere else in the city.

NORTH MELBOURNE

North Melbourne conceals the wonderfully preserved gold-rush-era streetscape of Errol Street (*see* box). Once part of Lieutenant-Governor La Trobe's original Royal Park reserve, North Melbourne was known as Hotham until 1887 and was best known as the home of the Melbourne Benevolent Asylum for the destitute and infirm from 1851 (it moved to Cheltenham in 1911) and as a departure point for the goldfields. The asylum's presence set the suburb's working class tone, though local educator Albert Mattingley wrote fondly of the suburb's 'park-like appearance, its carpet of grass and noble red gums'.

Land sales and subdivisions in the 1850s led to a rapid increase in population. Churches and schools quickly popped up, and by 1860 there were more than 7000 people living in the suburb. Residences varied greatly in quality: there were detached villas and ornate terraces (particularly on the high ground of Flemington Road) but elsewhere were large numbers of

ERROL STREET

SLEEPY ERROL Street evokes everyday 19th century Melbourne life like no other street in the city. Here you'll find numerous cafes and bars under wide verandahs full of laid-back locals enjoying their little hideaway just out of town. The 1890s depression had the effect of preserving North Melbourne's main street – basically freezing it in time.

Almost entirely intact from Victoria Street to Queensberry Street, it is dominated by the imposing 1876 North Melbourne Town Hall, designed by architect George Raymond Johnson in the Second Empire style. Johnson was a prolific architect of town halls; you can see his other work in Collingwood, Fitzroy and Northcote.

Included in Johnson's town hall complex was a court house, post office and five-storey clock tower. Out front is the North Melbourne drinking fountain with its ornamental kangaroo – a gift to the suburb from departing mayor Thomas Henderson in 1877. It had originally been located atop bluestone steps and surrounded by iron railings in the middle of the Errol and Queensberry street intersection, but was moved in 1889 to make way for cable tram tracks. Relocated to the footpath outside the town hall, it was damaged when hit by a car in 1972. In 2001 its drinking spout was fully restored to its 1877 design.

The town hall buildings' wide verandahs with corrugated iron roofs and cast-iron posts are replicated on both sides of the streets. This style – practical for its protection from sun and rain – was common across Victoria in the 19th century but was mostly removed during the mid 20th century to give towns and cities a more modern look.

A sip from this 1877 fountain is a vastly different experience to the Danks bubblers you might remember from school.

shabby timber cottages, as well as workshops, horse stables, tanneries, stores, factories and, later, the Hay Market and the Metropolitan Meat Market.

Based on Arden Street, the North Melbourne Football Club was formed in 1869 and the North Melbourne Town Hall, completed in 1876, signalled the suburb's prosperity. By the 1880s it had become the most densely populated part of the city. However, its low-lying parts were seriously overcrowded. The slum reclamation movement of the 1930s noted that some houses in laneways received just ten minutes of sunshine per day, and by the 1950s the Housing Commission had set about demolishing several blocks at the corner

THE LITTLE DOCTOR WILLIAM MALONEY

BORN IN West Melbourne in 1854, brought up by a single mother and schooled in North Melbourne, William Maloney was a local doctor for some 50 years. He travelled widely – joining the painters Tom Roberts and JP Russell on a walking tour of France and Spain in 1883 – and dressed in the bohemian fashion of the time: cream silk suit, bright bow-ties, panama hat and a waxed moustache. He opened his practice in North Melbourne in 1888 and in March the following year was elected to the Legislative Assembly for the seat of West Melbourne. It was the beginning of a 51-year stint as a Labor parliamentarian. He campaigned for women's suffrage (introducing the first ever women's suffrage bill into a British Empire parliament) as well as old-age and invalid pensions. When women's suffrage was finally achieved in 1908, 20,000 women signed an address of gratitude to him.

In 1896 he established a new practice at the Queen Victoria Market to treat the poor, and also supported early birth control campaigner Bessie Smyth. He entered federal politics in 1904 but, too easily distracted by causes close to his heart, was never a serious contender for ministerial positions. He continually campaigned for old-age and military pensions, maternity allowances and child endowments, and in 1935 even made a film appealing for milk for creches and free kindergartens. About a thousand people attended his 80th birthday celebration in 1934 and in 1940 he led the eight-hour day procession in recognition of his role as a Labor pioneer. Nicknamed the Little Doctor for his diminutive stature, he is believed to have been the illegitimate son of WJT 'Big' Clarke – pastoralist, politician and one of the wealthiest men of the Port Phillip district.

of Abbotsford and Haines streets and constructing the Haines Street walk-ups as well as the Melrose Street high-rise.

North Melbourne still retains its industrial heritage, with flour mills, an asphalt plant, cement mixing, storage, electricity generation and transport depots still operating despite an increasingly gentrified residential population moving in to converted warehouses.

Public Record Office Victoria

Tucked away in a suburban back street is the state's most important storage facility. Established under the *Public Records Act 1973*, the Public Record Office manages, preserves and provides access to the records of government and its agencies, such as public schools and hospitals, police, courts and other government institutions since 1836. It also stores collections of the National Gallery of Victoria (*see* p. 105) and Arts Centre. In the bowels of the Victorian Archives Centre there are about 100 kilometres of records, mainly documents and photographs, including petitions for women's suffrage and Aboriginal rights.

Bastow Institute of Educational Leadership

Education in North Melbourne had been pioneered by John Mattingley and his wife in 1857. Their son, Albert, taught at their school and later opened the Errol Street State School in 1874.

Designed by Henry Bastow in 1882, school no. 307 – now the Bastow Institute of Educational Leadership – honours the work of Henry Bastow and the *Education Act* 1872, which transformed education in Victoria by proclaiming it free, secular and compulsory. In just five years, Bastow oversaw the construction of 615 new schools in the state in what was the largest education building program ever undertaken in Australia.

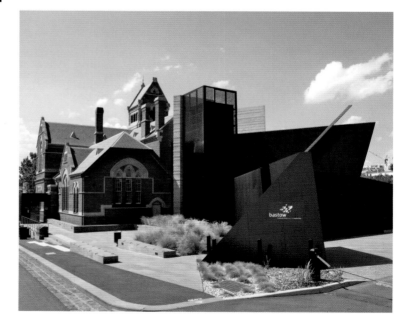

Cutting-edge architecture at the time of its construction in 1882, School No. 307 is now the Bastow Institute of Educational Leadership.

REDMOND BARRY

JUDGE AND cultural aesthete Redmond Barry played an important role in establishing key institutions in Melbourne. He was on the foundation committees that established the Melbourne Hospital in 1848, the University of Melbourne in 1853 and the Melbourne Public Library (now the State Library of Victoria) in 1854. He also judged the Eureka Stockade treason trials in 1855 (all were acquitted). When Barry sentenced bushranger Ned Kelly to death in 1880, Kelly replied that he would see him there. Barry died just twelve days after Kelly was hanged.

BACKGROUND The cloisters at the University of Melbourne, site of graduation day photos and the beginning of the eight-hour-day movement. **LEFT** Redmond Barry in his chancellor's robes. **RIGHT** Redmond Barry in his judge's robes.

Bushranger Ned Kelly is led to his death in 1880.

Old Melbourne Gaol

Melbourne's first gaol was constructed at the western end of Collins Street in 1839, where early punishments, mainly for drunkenness, included leg stocks. That site was abandoned in 1845 for a larger position at the corner of La Trobe and Russell streets, with the Supreme Court right next door. (The former Magistrates Court at the corner of La Trobe and Russell streets was built in 1914; there are numerous shrapnel marks from the 1986 Russell Street Bombing.)

As the colony boomed, stockades also became necessary. The first was in Carlton where Curtain Square is, itself a bluestone quarry. The stockade buildings have since been recycled into school buildings. Pentridge Prison (*see* p. 156) started in the exact same way, but by 1854 prison overcrowding required the use of prison hulks (*see* p. 167) in Hobsons Bay as well.

Continually expanded for decades, the gaol came to occupy an entire city block, bordered by a high bluestone wall. Male and female prisoners were co-located until a separate wing for women was opened in 1864. Homes for gaolers and warders were built inside the gaol as well as nearby on Franklin, Russell and Swanston streets.

By the time it closed in 1929, 133 people had been executed at the gaol by hanging. Tasmanian Aboriginal people Tunnerminnerwait and Maulboyheenner were the first to be hanged here, and bushranger Ned Kelly was the most infamous. The serial killer Frederick Bailey Deeming was hanged less than three months after the discovery of his third victim in 1892, and the Brunswick baby farmer Minnie Thwaites was hanged in 1894 for the murder of two babies found in her backyard. Each was buried – without their heads, according to law – in an unmarked grave within the gaol walls.

Whelan the Wrecker demolished part of the gaol in the early 1930s.

Today, the gaol has been partly incorporated into RMIT (the Royal Melbourne Institute of Technology), and the rest turned into a crime and justice museum, which displays the memorabilia of prisoners and staff, including death masks and even the tiny pencil used by the posthumously pardoned Colin Campbell Ross to protest his innocence before he was executed in 1922.

With the construction of the new Melbourne Museum next door, the Royal Exhibition Building became the largest item in the museum's collection.

Royal Exhibition Building

The enormous 1880 Royal Exhibition Building is Australia's only World Heritage Listed building. It is the world's best example of the opulent, extravagant and often ostentatious architecture of the International Exhibition movement that began in London in 1851.

EIGHT-HOUR DAY

STONEMASONS WORKING on Melbourne University's Old Quad downed tools on 21 April 1856 and marched to parliament house with other members of the building trade to protest for better working conditions. Until then, thanks to the Industrial Revolution, the working day could range from ten to 16 hours, sometimes six days a week, and child labour was common too. A public holiday was declared for 12 May 1856 (now celebrated as Labour Day on the second Monday in March), when about 700 people marched to the Cremorne Gardens (*see* p. 193) for a day of leisure. From 1879 the eight-hour day was declared a public holiday in Victoria and the practice instituted across the colony. An eight-hour day monument is located at the corner of Russell and Victoria streets, between Trades Hall and the Working Men's College, now RMIT.

MELBOURNE MUSEUM

THE MELBOURNE Museum is home to numerous Melbourne icons including an extensive local indigenous collection, the mounted hide of legendary racehorse Phar Lap, cable trams and old-fashioned traffic lights, as well as giant prehistoric animals Diprotodon and Muttaburrasaurus. The Biggest Family Album project collected almost 10,000 photos of Victorians from the 1890s to the 1940s, and the Marvellous Melbourne exhibition shows artefacts from Little Lon, Chinatown and Cole's Book Arcade in replica contexts.

These exhibitions were really the first international trade shows, and demonstrated advances in industry and technology. For Melburnians, it was a chance to show off.

Designed by Joseph Reed, the original building consisted of the Great Hall with its enormous dome (still extant) and numerous temporary annexes where the museum is now. Out front Josef Hochgurtel's ten-metre tall fountain symbolised the strong, proud young city. The exhibition was a great event for Melburnians and visitors, and almost 1.5 million visits were made between 1 October 1880 and 30 April 1881 – at the time there were just 250,000 people living in Melbourne. Gas lanterns throughout the building enabled night-time visits, and visitors could even take stairs to the dome for views across Marvellous Melbourne.

The building has been used for all kinds of exhibitions and major events, such as the 1888 Centennial Exhibition, the opening of the first Parliament of Australia and the unveiling of the competition-winning new Australian flag, both in 1901. The Victorian Parliament sat here for 27 years, and the annexes have also been used for bicycle racing, an emergency hospital during the 1919 influenza pandemic, air force barracks during World War II, a migrant hostel, a dance hall and even an aquarium. In 1956, the building hosted the Olympic basketball, weight lifting, wrestling and fencing competitions. The annexes, however, were not maintained and fell into disrepair and were either destroyed by fire or demolished. The building did not get its royal title until Princess Alexandra visited in 1984,

Cyclists cross Princes Street on the busy Canning Street bike path.

Italian Olympic gold-medal-winning cyclist Nino Borsari was competing in Australia when World War II broke out. Unable to return home he started a bicycle repair shop. The now heritage-listed neon sign was erected in the late 1940s at the corner of Lygon and Grattan streets.

usefully inspiring the restoration of the building and its interiors. The Great Hall and the surrounding Carlton Gardens have survived, and today play host to the Melbourne International Flower and Garden Show, markets, and all manner of expositions from the bridal to the building industries as well as high school and university exams.

Lygon Street

Stretching eight kilometres from Carlton through to Brunswick East, Lygon Street has long been famed as the home of Italian culture in Melbourne. You can see it brightest in the restaurant strip between Victoria and Elgin streets where you'll find scores of Italian restaurants, most with street-side al fresco seating and Italian-speaking waiters; but it's also in the concreted front yards and textile factories of Brunswick East. At the corner of Lygon and Faraday streets is King & Godfree – surely one of the oldest grocery stores in the country having operated there since 1884 and Italian-run since the 1920s.

Carlton locals owe their beautiful tree-lined median strip to the removal of cable trams in 1936. An engine house at Park Street has been converted to apartments.

Though Italians first came to Melbourne during the 1850s gold rush, it was the advent of fascism in Italy in the 1920s that precipitated the first wave of Italian migration to Australia, and the making of Little Italy around Lygon Street. The Italian community comes together for the annual Lygon Street Festa, and takes over Argyle Square, also known as Piazza Italia. The Musee Italiano provides a range of social services and documents the history of Italians in Australia.

Lygon Street's proximity to the university has made it popular among students and academics, and Melbourne's iconic Readings bookshop, the Nova arthouse cinema, Jimmy Watson's wine bar (renovated by the then emerging architect Robin Boyd in 1963), Brunetti cakes and La Mama Theatre have been local institutions for decades.

More than a million people are buried in the Melbourne General Cemetery, but grave sites still occasionally become available.

Melbourne General Cemetery

The Melbourne General Cemetery's establishment in 1853 facilitated the closure of the old Melbourne Cemetery on the site of the Queen Victoria Market. There are almost a million buried at the sprawling Carlton site, including many of the city's luminaries such as founding fathers John Pascoe Fawkner and Redmond Barry (*see* p. 138); Eureka Rebellion leader Peter Lalor; prime ministers James Scullin, Robert Menzies and John Gorton; explorers and companions in death Burke & Wills; the Princess Theatre's ghost Frederici Baker; and billiards champion Walter Lindrum, whose distinctive memorial is topped with a granite billiards table, cue and balls. Perhaps the most unexpected memorial is that to Elvis Presley, erected by the local Elvis Presley Fan Club just months after his death in 1977.

THE CARLTON CREW

IN THE late 1970s the Carlton Crew organised crime gang emerged with Alphonse Gangitano – 'The Black Prince of Lygon Street' – using stand-over tactics on the street's business owners and establishing himself as a drug trafficker. He was killed in 1998 – the first fatality in Melbourne's gangland killings. That escalated into a kind of war when rival trafficker Carl Williams was shot in the stomach in 1999 – and survived. Tit for tat murders resulted in 27 deaths by the time Williams was arrested in 2006. Sentenced to 35 years in prison in 2007, he was bashed to death in 2010. Widely reported in the press at the time, the Melbourne gangland killings were permanently etched into Melbourne folklore when the first *Underbelly* TV series screened in 2008.

MACROBERTSON'S WHITE CITY

JUST NEAR the corner of Argyle and Smith streets in Fitzroy is the general office of the former MacRobertson's chocolate factory. In his autobiography *A Young Man and a Nail Can*, Macpherson Robertson recounts how the business started out in the family's bathtub and grew into Australia's largest confectionery company with iconic chocolate bars Freddo Frog, Cherry Ripe and Old Gold. By the 1920s, he was one of the richest people in Australia. His factory complex, known as the White City, occupied two blocks of Fitzroy. Every day, approximately 2000 workers dressed in white would buzz about the white factory buildings, and white vans would deliver confectionery across the city. Robertson himself was also always impeccably dressed in white.

Robertson was also a generous philanthropist and innovator. To mark Melbourne's centenary he gifted £100,000 for the establishment of MacRobertson's Girls High School; the MacRobertson Bridge across the Yarra; the MacRobertson Fountain on the Domain and the Herbarium at the Royal Botanic Gardens. He was one of the first importers of bicycles to Australia, as well as chewing gum and fairy floss. He sponsored the first long haul aeroplane race between London and Melbourne and an around-Australia expedition, both as freight experiments, as well as Douglas Mawson's voyage to the South Pole, for which a vast chunk of Antarctica is named MacRobertsonland.

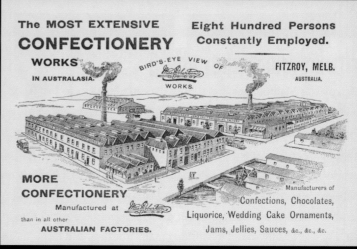

Employing about 2000 workers at the peak of production, MacRobertson's along with nearby Foy & Gibson's, was the country's largest employer of women.

By the 1920s, the state government accused the Fitzroy council of creating slums by allowing inappropriately small developments, such as three houses on a 31-foot by 100-foot block. In the 1960s the Housing Commission demolished hundreds of tenements and cottages at the corner of Brunswick and Gertrude streets to make way for the Atherton Gardens high-rise public housing estate, completed in 1972.

A bohemian scene emerged in the late 1970s, characterised by the Little Bands scene (think Ollie Olsen, Lisa Gerrard and Richard Lowenstein's *Dogs in Space*; 3RRR, which moved there from RMIT in 1979; and the Melbourne Fringe. Local institutions Marios and the Black Cat opened in the 1980s, and the Punters Club and the Evelyn became popular live music venues. Fitzroy remains a hub for live music and nightlife, particularly on Brunswick Street, but Gertrude Street has recently emerged as its hipper sister. Johnston Street is Melbourne's Hispanic enclave.

Australia's only saint, Mother Mary of the Cross MacKillop, was born in Fitzroy in 1842. Committed to poverty, she established the Sisters of St Joseph of the Sacred Heart, otherwise known as the Josephites, and set up schools for the rural poor throughout Australia. Her miracles include two cases of patients recovered from inoperable cancer.

FITZROY PUBS

FITZROY'S BACKSTREETS are dotted with pubs; in the late 19th century there were as many as 70 licenced hotels in the suburb. Competition was fierce, and local legend has it that a signboard for the pub Labour in Vain once portrayed a frustrated white woman labouring – in vain – to scrub the black off a black baby. Across the road, the Perseverance Hotel played one-upmanship: the black baby on their signboard was slowly turning white, thanks to her perseverance.

COLLINGWOOD AND ABBOTSFORD

The working class have always dominated Collingwood and Abbotsford. It began at the falls on the Yarra when John Dight bought 26 acres of surrounding land in 1839. The rock falls had long been used as a river crossing and a place to trap migrating fish, and the nearby confluence of the Merri Creek and Yarra River was a meeting place for Aboriginal peoples. In the early 1840s Dight built a water-powered flour mill on the site, which was in use until the 1900s. Numerous other mills operated in the area, notably the Yarra Woollen Mills and the 1888 polychrome brick Denton Hat Mills, designed by William Pitt. On Oxford Street in Collingwood was the enormous Gibsonia manufacturing complex, which supplied Foy & Gibson's department stores around the country. The Abbotsford Convent – built to accommodate a thousand girls – is sited on the longest continually farmed land in Port Phillip.

The residential blocks can be very small in these parts, though perhaps none smaller than 136 Sackville Street, where an 1850s prefabricated timber cottage still stands. Known as a Singapore Cottage, it was made in Singapore with instructions printed in Chinese on its parts to provide an easy onsite assembly guide. By contrast, the ornate 1887 Collingwood Town Hall is a fine example of 19th century civic architecture.

SQUIZZY TAYLOR

BORN IN Brighton, Squizzy Taylor was five years old when his family moved to Richmond in 1893 – the worst year of the depression. He grew up in Richmond and became the leader of a local gang, participated in the violent Fitzroy Vendetta and committed numerous offences. Starting out as a teenage pickpocket he quickly moved to burglary, bookmaking, sly-grog selling, extortion, prostitution, coke dealing, loitering and murder throughout the inner north. By the 1920s he was a showman gangster – and a household name. At just 5-foot, 2-inches he was a little fella but wielded a sharp tongue and a flair for mystery and surprise. He wrote letters to the media while he was in hiding from the police, during which time he even starred in a film about his life. Though he was rarely convicted of serious offences (thanks to a little luck and manipulation) he was killed in a gunfight in October 1927 with old foe John Snowy Cutmore. Though his influence had waned, his affinity for mystery had not; there are still unanswered questions about his death. The Nine Network TV series Underbelly: Squizzy has further embedded his story in Melbourne legend.

The rapids of Dight's Falls, still a popular fishing spot.

Since World War II, the area has become more socially and ethnically diverse. Victoria Street is particularly notable as the focus for Melbourne's largest Vietnamese community. Where before 1976 there had been only about 400 Vietnamese in Victoria, by 1981 there were 12,000. They came as 'boat people' – refugees who had fled war-torn Vietnam in the 1970s. Victoria Street is lined with Vietnamese restaurants, grocers and Asian import stores. Today there are more than 58,000 Vietnamese-born people in Victoria, and the surname Nguyen is the second-most listed name in Melbourne's phone directory after Smith.

Smith Street

In the 1870s, Smith Street emerged as one of the city's dominant shopping strips. Collingwood boomed along with the rest of Melbourne, and several grand buildings from bygone eras survive today, including John Marsden's Victorian Mannerist style Collingwood Post Office; Moran and Cato; Patterson's Emporium; and the Collingwood Coffee Palace, its facade barely concealing a carpark atop a Woolworths supermarket.

Foy & Gibson's opened here in 1883, basing their business on the famous Le Bon Marché in Paris. During the 1890s depression, Foy & Gibson's established woollen and hosiery mills on Oxford Street, employing 2000 people to make men's and ladies' clothing, hosiery, millinery, bedding and even furniture, hardware and food. Constructed to the design of William Pitt over several decades, the factory complex – known as Gibsonia – still dominates the area.

In 2010, more than 2000 people rallied to save local live music venue The Tote – a campaign that momentarily became a state election issue.

BRUNSWICK AND COBURG

Brunswick and Coburg were for years quarry sites, brickyards and open farmland. Surveyed in 1839 into long slender blocks between Moonee Ponds Creek (now under CityLink) and Merri Creek, Brunswick was first envisaged as agricultural properties served by a narrow road down the centre. You can still make out the original allotments on a map, though the narrow road now dominates thanks to the industry and commerce that continues to define these suburbs.

Brunswick first emerged as a town in the early 1840s with the building of Sydney Road. It got its first pub in 1842 when the Retreat Inn was built – run by a female publican – and by the end of the decade the road had been finished to Pentridge Prison (*see* p. 156) and the first brickworks had been established. From 1851 Brunswick grew as a pitstop for Collingwood and

The Hardwick Building, headquarters of Australian bridal designer Mariana Hardwick.

Fitzroy lads bound for the goldfields. A tent bazaar flourished, as did hardware and drapery stores and hotels. But it was the area's clay and bluestone that became the basis for its largest industries. Trams and trains came to the area in the 1880s and by the turn of the 20th century the suburb's clothing and textiles industries were being established. Europeans came after World War II, and more recently it has been migrants from Turkey and Lebanon.

Coburg was slower to develop. Named Pentridge in 1840 – before it got its eponymous prison – the area was originally home to vast farms, including John Pascoe Fawkner's and Dr Farquhar McCrae's (husband of the diarist Georgiana McCrae; their bluestone farmhouse La Rose, built in 1842, is the oldest private house in Victoria). Coburg's rich soils made it a profitable site for small farmers and market gardeners, plus it had even richer deposits of bluestone. The stigma of Pentridge Prison, however, led locals to petition for a new suburb name and in 1870 the name Coburg was bestowed in honour of Queen Victoria's husband, Prince Albert of Saxe-Coburg and Gotha.

The land boomers of the 1880s marketed Coburg as the Toorak of the north. Unfortunately it was speculators who purchased most of the allotments, and it wasn't until the 1910s that Coburg flourished as a suburb. The tranquil Merri Creek, with its artificial lake with

Chapter Six

WEST

PRISON HULKS

WITH SO many people coming to Victoria in search of gold, it was just a matter of time before Melbourne's prisons became overcrowded. And so in 1852 the government purchased the ship *President*, removing its masts and re-fitting it as a floating prison. But as the prison population continued to grow, so too did the fleet of prison hulks anchored in Hobson's Bay.

The hulks were intended to be a deterrent; certainly they were notorious for the cruelty inflicted on board. Prisoners were kept in irons below deck, sometimes in solitary confinement below the waterline, and punished with the cat o' nine tails. They worked daily quarrying bluestone on shore and building the breakwaters off the point. But just two years later there were more than 600 prisoners on the hulks, some as young as nine-years-old.

John Price, the Inspector General of Penal Establishments in charge of the hulks, was described by the *Age* as 'a man whose leading characteristics appear to be cunning and cruelty'. He was known for his violent punishments, and so it was no real surprise that when he went to Williamstown to hear the grievances of hulk prisoners that he was bashed to death with picks and shovels. An inquiry found that the brutality of the hulk system was the reason for the attack, but nevertheless it was 1885 before the Victorian government finally ordered the five prison hulks be broken up. The *Success*, however – requisitioned in 1854 after its crew abandoned it for the goldfields – survived until 1945 touring the world as 'the famous Australian convict ship'. Aboard were wax figures wearing prison clothes and irons demonstrating the stories of convict life on the hulks.

An anchor believed to belong to one of the prison hulks was found in 1990 and is now located next to the Timeball Tower at Point Gellibrand. At the National Sports Museum at the MCG is an old bell from the prison hulk *Lysander*. It has signalled the news of Separation from New South Wales, warned of escapees from Pentridge and been used by fire brigades in Coburg and Richmond. From 1922 'Old Lysander' was used to sound the start and end of every quarter of footy played at the 'G until the siren was introduced in 1948.

on the pier in 1859 – the water and fish underneath
usefully carrying away the mess of autopsy.

By 1861 Williamstown had 13 slips for boat
repairs and building, and pier accommodation for
40 vessels. New ships – some in excess of 2000
tonnes – could not navigate the Yarra and so had to lie
at anchor in Hobson's Bay, so by 1870 Williamstown
had become the major cargo port of Victoria with its
local population almost entirely employed in shipping
industries. New docks and slipways included Victoria's first and the country's largest dry dock –
its foundation stone laid by Prince Alfred on his 1868 tour – still in use today.

*The view from Williamstown's
Gem Pier with the city rising in
the background.*

The Blunt family's boatyard and slipway has operated on Nelson Place since the 1880s
(and since the late 1850s in Geelong), a solitary reminder of the many small boat-building
businesses that once occupied the area. But it's the Williamstown Naval Dockyards that
dominate the foreshore, even though they're mostly inaccessible. Numerous Australian Navy
vessels have been built here, including the World War II minesweeper *HMAS Castlemaine*, now
a floating museum on Gem Pier. Private companies now operate from the site, where vessels for
the Royal Australian Navy are still built.

In 1908, 22 ships of the US Navy visited. Known as the Great White Fleet, they were on
a circumnavigation of the globe in what was the greatest demonstration of naval power during
peacetime ever seen. During the subsequent Fleet Week celebrations, a collision occurred
between the *USS Ajax* and a crowded sightseeing boat, the *SS Leura*. No lives were
lost and both were repaired, though the *USS Ajax* required a new stern, 19 metres
long, to be constructed and fitted.

*The ornate Wilkinson Memorial
Drinking Fountain with its
British bulldogs.*

The Commonwealth Reserve is also the site of the convict-built 1857 Tide
Gauge House (originally located at Point Gellibrand), which housed a tide
gauge that helped determine the Australian Height Datum; the 1875 Wilkinson
Memorial Drinking Fountain, an ornate fountain honouring local teetotaller and
Anglican Reverend George Wilkinson who sought to give sailors and sightseers
alternative options to refreshments at the town's pubs; and the anchor of the
126-gun *HMS Nelson*, the first ship to dock in the completed Alfred Graving

Point Gellibrand is named for Joseph Tice Gellibrand, Hobart lawyer and founding member of the Port Phillip Association, who disappeared in 1837 while exploring Melbourne's hinterland. His body has never been found.

Dock. Across the road at 1 Parker Street, the 1860 Williamstown Post Office (now a restaurant) is the oldest post office building still standing in Victoria.

Point Gellibrand

Point Gellibrand guards the entrance to the mouth of the Yarra. It has been a quarry, a quarantine station, a cemetery, telegraph station, fort, railway and shipbuilding yards, and is today a coastal heritage park.

In 1842, the appearance of the ship *Manlius* threw the small colony into a frenzy. The ship's immigrants were part of a British labour scheme that paid captains a bounty to deliver passengers in good health. The captain of the *Manlius* – now known as the plague ship – would not receive his bounty as 45 of the ship's 243 passengers had died from yellow fever en route from Scotland. The remaining passengers were taken to a hastily erected quarantine camp at the point, where 17 more died. All were buried at Point Gellibrand, which also served as the

NEUTRALITY OR NUISANCE?

IN 1865, Melbourne had its first visit from an active warship. After sailing from the Confederate States Navy's unofficial home port of Liverpool, the *Shenandoah* made numerous successful attacks on Union merchant ships in the Indian Ocean before sailing into Hobson's Bay on 25 January 1865. The Captain JI Waddell sought repairs, food and water, but the Victorian government was concerned that their neutrality would be compromised if they allowed the ship to dock. So they rented one of their docks to a private firm, who in turn allowed the ship to dock.

Though only a day or two was needed for repairs, the *Shenandoah* stayed a month. Melburnians came in droves for a stickybeak. Fearing British subjects were being recruited, the US Consul called for the ship's captain to be arrested. Victorian soldiers and police searched the ship on several occasions, and Captain Waddell even offered to surrender the ship to the British Crown. That too would be a compromise of neutrality, and the government would have nothing of it. But it did buy enough time to finish repairs and get the ship back in the water. In the end, 42 men were recruited in Melbourne and 19 crew deserted. The *Shenandoah* went on to capture dozens of Union vessels, mainly whalers, before Captain Waddell heard the news of General Lee's surrender in August 1865. The *Shenandoah*'s flag was the last sovereign Confederate flag to be furled after she was surrendered in Liverpool's Mersey River on 6 November 1865. At an 1871 hearing of the International Court in Geneva, the British Government was ordered to pay £820,000 to the US government for allowing the use of the port at Williamstown.

Built by convicts in 1849, Williamstown Lighthouse is Victoria's second-oldest. The anchor at its base is believed to come from one of the old prison hulks.

cemetery for deceased convicts from the prison hulks, sailors and residents of Williamstown.

The fort was completed in 1855, though the Russian invasion that inspired its construction never eventuated, and there is no evidence that Russian vessels were ever even in the area. Regular additions and improvements were made over the following decades, but by the 1890s the fort's importance diminished as the colony's defence system concentrated at Port Phillip Heads (*see* p. 234). There were a few close calls with passing ships during firing practice, but the fort was never used in anger. It became an artillery test range in the 1930s and was last in use during World War II. When the Williamstown Cricket Club recently excavated to install an underground water tank, a brick bunker and tunnel were uncovered, believed to have been built in the 1850s – making it the oldest remaining defence installation in Victoria.

Built from bluestone quarried by convicts just a few hundred metres away in 1849, the Williamstown Lighthouse at Point Gellibrand is the second oldest lighthouse in Victoria. The unusual square tower – just seventeen metres tall – replaced an 1840 timber structure and other navigational aids. From March 1854, this was also the location of the first telegraph line in Australia, which operated between Melbourne and Williamstown.

It only operated as a lighthouse until 1859, when lightships were used to guard the reefs off Point Gellibrand, at which time it became a time ball tower. The large ball that still sits atop the tower was dropped at 1pm each day so that ships' masters moored in the bay could correct their chronometers. By the 1930s that technology had also been superseded. The brightening light of the city had also made the lightships less effective, so the tower was re-established as a lighthouse, in use until 1987.

In 1857 the Victorian government built its first railway from Point Gellibrand to Spencer Street, locating its workshops over a vast area of the point. Railway workers were busily employed in the construction, repair and maintenance of trains – initially assembling imported steam locomotives, and later building their own. In 1889 new workshops were established just up the line at Newport, and while the Williamstown workshops have closed, the Newport ones are still used today.

Wreckage of the Westgate Bridge following its collapse in 1970.

Westgate Bridge Memorial Park

The 2.5 kilometre Westgate Bridge is a crucial link in Melbourne's transport network. When it was completed in 1972, it was envisaged to carry 40,000 vehicles per day. In 2014 it averaged upwards of 200,000 per day. The giant Australian and Victorian flags flown atop the bridge's masts cost $350,000 to install and $15,000 a year to maintain.

While still under construction in 1970, the span between piers 10 and 11 collapsed, killing 35 construction workers – most of whom were crushed to death while they were on lunch break in the workers huts below the bridge. It's said that the crash could be heard 20 kilometres away. The Royal Commission into the accident found that 80 tonnes of concrete used to rectify a gap between the spans caused them to buckle and collapse. Twisted fragments of the bridge are now in the gardens of Monash University's engineering faculty at Clayton, serving to remind students of the consequences of their errors.

Despite the surrounding industry, the rivermouth is still a popular fishing spot.

MARVELLOUS SMELLBOURNE

A KEY component of Melbourne's long-awaited sewerage system, the 1897 Spotswood Pumping Station played the crucial role of pumping sewage up rising mains to join the main sewer outfall where it would flow under gravity to the Werribee Treatment Farm, some 25 kilometres away.

It was a project that sought to resolve the dichotomy of Melbourne's two nicknames: Marvellous Melbourne and Marvellous Smellbourne. Where the former referred to the grand buildings and stately boulevards, the latter conveyed its lack of this most basic infrastructure. Open gutters in the street carried sewage, storm water, horse manure, and all manner of industrial waste into the creeks and rivers. The stench would have been horrible.

Built at the height of the 1890s depression, the sewerage system – the largest infrastructure project then undertaken – provided much-needed jobs and was a vital boost to the local economy. Melbourne's rapid growth following the Second World War meant that the station's capacity was soon exceeded, so a new pumping station was built further west at Brooklyn. Having carried all of Melbourne's waste for almost 70 years, the Spotswood complex was decommissioned in 1965.

Heritage-listed in 1981, the Spotswood Pumping Station and its unique collection of engineering equipment including tools and furniture buildings, and WWII air raid shelters, are now part of Museum Victoria's Scienceworks interactive science and technology centre.

It's less than ten minutes into the city by train from Footscray.

FOOTSCRAY

With its markets and transport hub, and location close to the CBD, Footscray is the unofficial capital of the west. It is a melting pot of culture, chock full of restaurants, grocers, languages and aromas from all over the world, each reflecting successive waves of migrants that found a new start in Melbourne's industrial heartland. Asians and Africans are particularly prominent as the most recent arrivals; the influence of southern Europeans having waned in recent years. Approximately 25 per cent of the population is from Asia; most notable in the dominance of Vietnamese restaurants in downtown Footscray.

It was 1839 when a punt crossed the Maribyrnong River – to provide a shortcut between Melbourne and the fledgling settlements of Ballarat and Geelong – and Footscray was born. The Punt Hotel was soon operating, its clientele made up of drovers transporting cattle to Melbourne's hinterland. After 1851, the pub did a roaring trade with gold diggers.

Connected by rail to the city and Williamstown in 1857, industry flourished. The land yielded bluestone while the river served to transport the product (and waste) of Footscray's burgeoning boiling down works, tanneries and wool scourers. In the process, Footscray earned itself two nicknames: Stoneopolis and Stinkopolis. Nearby in Maribyrnong, Pipemakers Park reveals these and other industrial histories. While factories and warehouses are still in Footscray, many former industrial sites are being transformed into housing estates.

Footscray is set for rapid expansion in the coming decades. In the five years to 2011 nearly 9000 additional dwellings were built in Footscray, and many thousands more are planned across multi-million dollar, multi-storey residential tower developments that will transform the suburb into a high-density urban area. For now, Footscray retains its grungy feel; the gleaming glass towers of Melbourne still a glimmer in the distance.

Pipemakers Park

Next door to Highpoint Shopping Centre is the Pipemakers Park living history museum. Here in the late 1840s was one of Melbourne's earliest manufacturing industries – a boiling down works. It was a gruesome business reducing animal carcasses to tallow, then loading it onto barges for processing into candles down river. By the 1860s, a meat cannery was operating here – producing more than half of all canned meat exported to Britain from Australia. The rough bluestone buildings, from a quarry now underneath Highpoint, still stand. By 1910, the Hume Brothers Cement Iron Factory was busily innovating the field of pre-cast concrete – manufacturing the world's first steel-reinforced concrete pipes.

The 16-metre statue of the Chinese seafarers' deity Mazu adorns a 33-square metre temple site at a bend in the Maribyrnong. It's so far been more than a decade in the making – built entirely with donations – and includes a garden, drum tower, lake pavilion, exhibition centre and a jetty.

ACTIVISM

FOOTSCRAY RESIDENTS have a long and proud history of lobbying and activism. From Aboriginal rights leaders to local councillors lobbying to bring industry to Footscray, to youth workers and LGBTI campaigners, Footscray's working class population unites for the common cause. You can see it in the fight for a minimum wage in 1907 (*see* box, p. 183), the response to the outbreak of war in 1914 and numerous industrial disputes since.

Among the activists are William Cooper, an Aboriginal rights leader who in 1938 organised the Day of Mourning to commemorate the sesquicentenary of colonisation, a protest that led to the establishment of NAIDOC Week in 1940 and continues today. Cooper also organised the world's only protest against Kristallnacht – the Nazi Night of Broken Glass. Trees have been planted in Jerusalem in his honour and the footbridge at Footscray Station bears his name.

Peter Tatchell, primarily a gay and lesbian rights advocate, campaigned against the hanging of Ronald Ryan in 1967 by painting slogans around Footscray, and in 1968 was involved in Aboriginal land rights. His school headmaster illogically claimed he had been manipulated by communists. He moved to England in 1971 to avoid conscription into the army, helped establish London's first Pride March in 1972 and became a leading member of the gay rights group OutRage! He has twice attempted a citizens arrest on Zimbabwean president Robert Mugabe.

The Footscray Ratepayers Vigilance Association formed in 1933 to protest the demolition and construction of a new town hall. While they weren't successful, the town hall that was built is a rare example of Richardsonian Romanesque Revival architecture that features a mix of Art Deco, Moderne, French, Spanish and Italian medieval styles.

Kinnears Rope Works with their display stand made of rope at the 1880 Melbourne International Exhibition.

The 1878 Jack's Magazine provided bonded storage for gunpowder and explosives imported to Victoria. Designed by government architect William Wardell, it features two bluestone vaulted buildings entirely concealed behind earthen blast walls and connected to the river by canal. It ultimately determined the location of munitions production in Victoria, with the Footscray Munitions Factory built next door in 1888 by the Colonial Ammunition Company of New Zealand, later purchased by the Australian government. Munitions made here were used for domestic military training and the police force, specifically 0.303 rifles. The name Jack's is said to refer to the 1920s magazine keeper Wally Jack.

YARRAVILLE AND SEDDON

Yarraville and Seddon have long been working class suburbs, though their proximity to town means they are experiencing rapid gentrification. Local communities in both suburbs have fought fiercely for their independence from neighbouring Footscray. The Seddon we know today did not fully exist until the early 20th century, so it was for a time known as Footscray South. But where Footscray bustles Seddon hushes.

Yarraville is on slightly higher ground and was initially promoted as a rural retreat. The selling agents Biers, Henningham & Co. threw a banquet lunch to launch land sales in 1859, extolling the views and fresh country air, though without a train station until 1871 its isolation meant it really only attracted local quarry, factory and waterside workers. Thereafter, housing boomed, attracting all manner of industry men including engineers, chemists, rope-weavers and more. Shops and business clustered on Anderson and Ballarat streets, around Yarraville Station. Its wharves were even busier than Footscray, servicing timber and oil industries, woollen, acid and bone mills, and the Colonial Sugar Refining Company.

In the early 20th century, the Yarraville Progress Association and the Yarraville Vigilance Association formed, and Yarraville maintained its own local newspapers. A tram through Footscray and Seddon to Williamstown Road in 1921 (since removed) encouraged house building and with it a particularly tight local community. During the Great Depression, locals

Before Seddon was named for a local lad who went on to become New Zealand's longest-serving prime minister (sometimes known as King Dick), it was called Belgravia. The 1875 Belgravia Hotel – where the Footscray Football Club is said to have been formed – is the last remaining building carrying the suburb's former name.

YARRAVILLE MOUTH ORGAN BAND

YARRAVILLE'S COMMUNITY spirit is perhaps most evident in the 80-year-old Yarraville Mouth Organ Band. It was formed in 1933 by Ern Weybury 'to keep the young people off the street' during the Depression; its first harmonicas supplied free by a local music shop. Within two years they'd won the B-Grade Championship. But from a competition that once included 35 bands, Yarraville is the only one remaining in Victoria.

organised to help the unemployed and promoted local shopping. Today, Yarraville's village atmosphere has attracted a new professional class to renovate its charming Victorian- and Edwardian-era backstreets.

The Sun Theatre

The Sun Theatre became a focal point for the community when it was built in 1938, and by the 1960s reflected the suburb's changing demographic by showing Greek language films. But television soon killed the cinema, and the Sun closed in 1982. Yarraville's local spirit, however, soon shined again with a multicultural festa and renewed appreciation for its heritage village feel. By the 1990s, the Sun had been restored and reopened as a multiplex, and in 2012 the street out front of the cinema was converted into a public park. The surrounding streets now hum with restaurants, bars and cafes.

No matter the weather or time of day, the Sun shines in Yarraville.

ALTONA

The Altona suburbs take in the Altona Coastal Park to the east, the Cheetam Wetlands to the west and stretch to the Westgate Freeway in the north. The Hobson's Bay Coastal Trail shared cycling and walking track connects from Williamstown to Werribee. At Altona, it loops around Cherry Lake, and is a great way to get a good look at this suburb.

Though it didn't get its first post office until 1918, the first homestead was established in 1842 and the suburb named by Frederick Taegtow after his home town of Altona in Germany. By 1861 the name had stuck. Taegtow went on to form a coal prospecting company, and a mine operated from what is now Harrington Square Shopping Centre until the 1920s when the La Trobe Valley open-cut mine was established.

The Altona region is also the home of early flight (*see* box) in Australia. Today it's most well known for the maze of pipes, chimneys, tanks and the eternal flame of the Altona oil refinery – still operating despite most of the industry relocating to Asia. When Toyota's Altona car manufacturing plant closes at the end of 2017 it will mark the end of car making in Australia.

Altona Coastal Park

The Altona Coastal Park including Cherry Lake points to the area's naturally marshy nature, while Racecourse Road remembers the Williamstown racecourse, which operated here from 1870 until 1940, when racing ceased and it became an army camp during World War II. A disastrous fire in 1947 meant the racecourse was never reopened. Instead, the army camp became the site of the Williamstown Migrant Hostel in 1949 – one among many for the hundreds of thousands of displaced persons and assisted immigrants who came to Australia after the war. The ruins of the racecourse grandstand are still visible.

THE MAGIC OF FLYING

THE AMERICAN magician and escapologist Harry Houdini made the first powered flight in Australia in nearby Diggers Rest in 1910, and later that year Frenchman Gaston Cugnet flew a Bleriot monoplane at Altona. Crucially, Altona was flat and barely populated, with only about 50 people living in the area. Cugnet hit a cow on landing but confidently advertised he would fly again the following week, inviting the public to watch. Strong winds prevented the demonstration, which angered the 3000-strong crowd – each of whom had paid an admission fee and for the train or steamer trip. In a letter to the Melbourne press, Cugnet noted that attempting to fly in the conditions would have risked injury 'to the only machine we have in Australia'. The *Advertiser* responded, 'Well if this wind can stop a flying machine, nobody but a Frenchman would get excited about such an invention.' Flying continued of course, and on 20 February 1911 JJ Hammond flew solo from Altona to Geelong, and on 23 February undertook the first powered passenger flight in the country.

In 1914 the Australian Flying Corps (later to become the Royal Australian Air Force or RAAF) established its training school at Point Cook, still in operation today. The RAAF also maintains a base at Laverton.

WERRIBEE

Located 32 kilometres from Melbourne, Werribee is one of the largest and fastest-growing suburbs in Australia and testament to the extent of the city's urban sprawl. Werribee is famed for its open-range safari-style zoo, a stately mansion, and a sewerage treatment farm. Established as an agricultural settlement in the 1850s and originally named Wyndham, it was renamed Werribee in 1904 after local squatters the Chirnside Brothers' Werribee Park estate.

Surrounded by thousands of hectares of conservation reserve, including one of the last unmodified areas of saltmarsh on Port Phillip, it is one of Australia's best-known sites for birdwatching. About 270 species of bird have been recorded here, and it is one of the few wintering sites for the critically endangered Orange-bellied Parrot.

Werribee Park

Werribee Park encompasses the Chirnside Brothers' 1877 Italianate mansion with its heritage orchard and rose gardens as well as the modern Werribee Open Range Zoo. Thomas and Andrew Chirnside were wealthy squatters who came to the Port Phillip district from Scotland in 1839. They settled first at Point Cook, though they built several homesteads across their vast portfolio.

Andrew began building Werribee Park Mansion in 1874 for his wife and young family. When it was completed three years later it was composed of 60 rooms with a central tower overlooking vast landscaped gardens. Thomas joined them there in 1877, and together they controlled some 200,000 acres and hundreds of workers across numerous runs. They bred Hereford cattle and imported foxes, hares, pheasants and partridges, as well as red deer for hunting. Manorial in their management approach, no one worked on Sundays and regular parties and picnics were given – at which it is said that Thomas's appearance on horseback would be greeted by cheers. By 1884, however, Thomas had grown increasingly depressed. He transferred most of his estate to his brother and nephews, and believed himself to be bankrupt. He shot himself in 1887; his estate was sworn for probate at more than £100,000.

Werribee Treatment Farm

The Melbourne Metropolitan Board of Works (MMBW) was formed in 1891 to manage water supply and sewage treatment. A treatment farm was built at Werribee and a pumping station was built at Spotswood (*see* p. 171). At a time when most cities dumped their waste untreated directly into rivers and the sea, the engineers of the MMBW designed an innovative broad irrigation system large enough to last 50 years. It began with a water closet at every property, which delivered the sewage by gravity through a network of underground sewers of increasing diameter to a steam pumping station at Spotswood, where it was forced up wrought iron rising mains to Brooklyn to begin its 25-kilometre journey along the Main Outfall Sewer to Werribee. The first property connected to the system was the All England Eleven Hotel in Rouse Street, Port Melbourne. Werribee Farm handled all of Melbourne's waste treatment until a second treatment plant was built at Carrum in 1975.

Thomas and Andrew Chirnside's enormous Werribee Park, showing the ornamental rose garden.

THE MELBOURNE CUP

THE ANNUAL Spring Racing Carnival – cleverly timed between football and cricket season – attracts around 400,000 people a year; more than 100,000 attend Flemington on Melbourne Cup Day alone. The Victoria Derby is the carnival's oldest race, but it's the Melbourne Cup – first run in 1861 – that is its most famous.

Held on the first Tuesday of November, the Melbourne Cup is known as the race that stops a nation. That's true even for people who don't follow horse racing, as a public holiday has commemorated the race since 1877, and Melburnians gather in backyards and huddle around TVs in the same way as they do on AFL Grand Final Day. Those interstate at least stop to watch the race and determine the winners of the sweepstakes, and perhaps indulge in a champagne lunch too. The Melbourne Cup was the brainchild of Captain Frederick Charles Standish, chief commissioner of police and member of the Victoria Racing Club. A grandstand was built in 1873, and as the course flourished so too did rose gardens, lawns, the betting ring and the birdcage – all of which have become as famous as the race itself.

The Melbourne Cup has prize money exceeding $6.4 million and is one of the richest horse races in the world, and has also attracted many myths. Archer was the first horse to win – and returned to win the following year. Legend had it that Archer and his jockey walked the 800 kilometres from Sydney, but they actually came by steamer. The Cup's most famous winner, Phar Lap, took out the race in 1930. He had to be hidden before the race after someone had tried to shoot him. Of course, Phar Lap died mysteriously in the US in 1932 – possibly from arsenic poisoning. Makybe Diva is the only horse to have won the Cup three times – in 2003, 2004 and 2005.

TOP Phar Lap winning the 1930 Melbourne Cup.

FLEMINGTON

Flemington and its neighbouring suburbs of Kensington and Ascot Vale are all closely associated with horse racing, and many street names reference famous racecourses. The first race meet was held on the future site of the Flemington Racecourse in March 1840, and the first land sales held in December of the same year. Flemington's name derives from the home town in Scotland of one of the first buyers.

With the discovery of gold in 1851, what had been the main road to Sydney suddenly became the more important road to the Mount Alexander goldfields, hence the current name. For a time Flemington and Kensington flourished on the needs of passing gold seekers; however, their proximity to the Maribyrnong made the location ideal for the noxious trades and so by the 1860s there were abattoirs, mills, candle works and tanneries all operating in close proximity to the Flemington Racecourse. Yes it would have been stinky. North of the racecourse, Ascot Vale was settled into small 50-acre farms.

The racecourse brought trains and trams to the neighbourhood early. The Melbourne and Essendon Railway Company opened their line through Newmarket to Essendon in 1860, and built a branch line to Flemington Racecourse in time for the first Melbourne Cup in 1861. Residential development began in the 1880s, mostly around the train lines. In Ascot Vale, a Temperance Township Estate was built between Union, Maribyrnong and Epsom roads – with owners prevented from distilling, brewing and serving alcohol on site. In 1882, new showgrounds were established north of the racecourse.

Development continued in the 20th century around the tram line between North Melbourne and the Maribyrnong at Ascot Vale. In the 1960s, the Housing Commission built high-rises at Debney's Paddock, formerly a tannery, then a rubbish tip and now a park overshadowed by the CityLink sound tunnel. With the flats came migrants from southern Europe, Asia and these days Africa, providing the Racecourse Road village with fresh flavour.

Flemington's ornate post office.

Erected in 1977 as advertising for Four 'n' Twenty Pies, the Pie in the Sky has been a meeting place for generations of Melburnians attending the Royal Melbourne Show.

Apartment towers loom over Moonee Ponds' 19th century streetscape.

MOONEE PONDS AND BEYOND

When we think of Melbourne's west we often think west of the Maribyrnong to the bay at Werribee. But that is to the exclusion of our friends in Moonee Ponds, Essendon and Keilor, who are today almost ensnared by CityLink and the Western Ring Road.

At Keilor is Victoria's most significant Aboriginal archaeological site (*see* p. 184), Essendon was the site of the city's first international airport, and Moonee Ponds – originally Moonee Moonee Ponds, after a chain of waterholes that once fed into the West Melbourne Swamp – is the home of Australia's most famous housewife, Dame Edna Everage (*see* box).

Farmers established themselves on land between the Maribyrnong and Moonee Ponds Creek in 1840 and by 1848 had formed the Port Phillip Farmers' Society – the first incarnation of the Royal Agricultural Society of Victoria, which throws the city's annual Royal Melbourne

DAME EDNA EVERAGE

BORN IN Wagga Wagga, Edna Everage first played to audiences in 1955. She introduced herself as 'Everage as in "average", husband Norm as in "normal",' and an interview with Mrs Everage from Moonee Ponds was one of the first screened on Channel 7's first day of programming in 1956. But Edna was made for the world, particularly after she was made a Dame by Gough Whitlam at the end of the 1974 film *Barry McKenzie Holds His Own*. Dame Edna soon found her way into the hearts of many with her trademark welcome 'Hello Possums!', cats' eye 'face furniture', arms full of gladdies, and a series of chat shows that satirise celebrity, snobbery and prudishness. She is still playing to audiences after 60 years, and is remembered in Dame Edna Place off Little Collins Street in central Melbourne.

THE SUN SHINES ON THE MINIMUM WAGE

FURTHER WEST the suburb of Sunshine – first known as Braybrook Junction – pays homage to HV McKay's Sunshine Harvester Works, and with it the birth of the minimum wage in Australia. McKay moved his agricultural machinery manufacturing business here in 1906, and built it up to become the largest manufacturing plant in Australia. He also bought the surrounding 400 acres, encouraging his workers to settle the area and providing electric street lighting, parks and sports grounds, a school, library, amenities for a pipe band and of course hundreds of jobs. After just one year an industrial dispute between McKay and his workers led to the Harvester Judgement, the benchmark industrial decision that led to the creation of a minimum living wage for Australian workers. From then on, Australia's minimum wage was based on what was fair and reasonable rather than what the employer was offering. In Justice Higgins' own words, the test of a fair and reasonable wage was 'the normal needs of the average employee regarded as a human being living in a civilised community'. He also said that the pay of the employee should not be dependent on the profits of the employer. The wage was set at £2 2s per week – the amount an average worker paid for food, shelter and clothing for him and his family.

Show. The 1850s brought gold seekers right through their district, with stopovers at the Moonee Ponds junction on Mount Alexander Road as well as at philanthropist Caroline Chisholm's family shelters (*see* box, p. 184) at Essendon, Keilor and beyond.

The Melbourne and Essendon Railway Company brought trains to Essendon in 1860, eventually connecting all the way to Wodonga on the Victoria and New South Wales border. Puckle Street between the train line and the Mount Alexander Road junction became the area's commercial centre, while Essendon grew as a rural retreat hidden between the meat works of Flemington, the brickworks of Brunswick and the factories of Footscray. Duplication of the railway lines and new tram routes in the early 20th century brought even more residents – and with them a community spirit to clean up the polluted Saltwater River, lining its banks with trees and renaming it the Maribyrnong. All the while, this hidden valley has remained a tranquil suburban getaway.

CAROLINE CHISHOLM

FOR MANY gold seekers, the gold rush was actually a very long walk – 100 kilometres from Melbourne to Ballarat. But this wasn't the El Camino with towns every few kilometres for rest or respite from heat, rain, wind or cold. Humanitarian and philanthropist Caroline Chisholm soon changed that. Arriving in Australia in 1838, Caroline Chisholm was concerned for the young women arriving in the colony with no money, friends, family or even jobs to go to. So she established homes for female immigrants to help them transition to a new life in the colonies. When she toured the Victorian goldfields in 1854, she found it an inhospitable trek unsuitable for families, which led to a gross imbalance of the sexes and its attendant social problems. Her answer was to construct family shelter sheds a day's walk apart from one another all the way to the goldfields. Two of these sheds were located on the Keilor Plains, both since gone. She also founded the Family Colonization Loan Society, which helped immigrant families pay their fare to Australia to establish new lives. Charles Dickens is said to have based the character of Mrs Jellyby in *Bleak House* on Caroline Chisholm.

Brimbank Park

Brimbank Park in Keilor is a vast green wedge where the Maribyrnong doubles back on itself some 50 metres below the Keilor Plain and where Taylors Creek drains through the Green Gully. Here you can encounter river red gums, ancient river fords, stone ruins and scar trees and an archaeological site where the 14,500-year-old Keilor Cranium was found in 1940, and the 7500-year-old Green Gully Skeleton, found in 1965.

Subsequent archaeological digs have uncovered stone artefacts as well as megafauna that lived in these parts as long as 40,000 years ago, including the giant possum Thylacoleo and the two-metre-tall wombat Diprotodon.

Tullamarine Airport

Construction of Melbourne's international airport at Tullamarine began in 1964 and the airport officially opened in 1970, replacing Essendon Airport as the city's international airport and introducing 'Tulla' into the city's lexicon. Tullamarine is named for Tullamareena, a Wurundjeri elder believed to have been at John Batman's attempted land purchase in 1835 (*see* p. 16). In 1838 Tullamareena was arrested for sheep stealing and imprisoned in the Melbourne Gaol on Collins Street. As police magistrate William Lonsdale described, Tullamareena escaped after he drew a long piece of reed from the gaol's thatch roof, lit it on the guard's candle and set the wooden prison on fire. He was recaptured again and sent for trial in Sydney, but released without charge and was not subsequently recorded in government documents.

More than 30 million passengers passed through Tulla in 2014, and this number is expected to more than double by 2030. In that time, the airport is expected to spend more than $10 billion on upgrades. The airport's 14-storey Air Traffic Control tower, built in 1969, was the first of its kind in Australia and is now heritage-listed.

Watercolourist Wilbraham Frederick Liardet's crude depiction of Tullamareena escaping the first Melbourne gaol in 1838 by cleverly setting it on fire.

Chapter Seven

EAST

RICHMOND AND CREMORNE

HAWTHORN AND KEW

CAMBERWELL AND CANTERBURY

BOX HILL, BALWYN, BULLEEN AND BEYOND

THE DANDENONGS

MELBOURNE'S EAST IS the epicentre of middle class Melbourne.

Most of the city's elite private schools are located in the inner east, as well as many of the city's most desirable addresses, such as Hawthorn, Kew and Canterbury. Demonstrating Melbourne's tendency for development towards the south-east, Glen Iris became the geographic centre of Melbourne in the 1990s. Two quintessential dramatisations of urban life in Melbourne are also set here – the World War II era *The Sullivans* (*see* box, p. 202) as well as the contemporary *Neighbours*, previously starring Melbourne's most famous daughter, Kylie Minogue (*see* box, p. 201) – herself brought up in Camberwell and about as middle class Melbourne as you could get.

While Richmond and Cremorne – with their narrow streets, single fronted cottages and criss-cross of trams – reflect life in the 19th century, the middle- and outer-east were largely developed in the 20th century and were post World War II the purest expression of the Australian Dream: a quarter-acre block, a Holden out the front and a hills hoist out the back.

But before all this the area had been fairly forested with Stringybark, Box, Candlebark and Manna Gum, and was the home territory of the Wurundjeri people. It was not particularly attractive to pastoralists, and for that reason you can still see rare shiny wallaby grass at Burwood East's Highbury Park. By the mid 19th century, river and creek gullies were under cultivation by orchardists and horticulturalists; and cut flowers were still being grown at Burwood until the 1950s.

The famed Heidelberg School artists (*see* p. 204) painted at numerous sites throughout the north-east in the late 19th century, and the Heide Circle (*see* p. 204) gathered at Bulleen from the 1930s. Monsalvat (*see* p. 205) in Eltham is still a working artists' colony. Further east, among the trees of the Dandenong Ranges (*see* p. 207) is one of Melbourne's favourite hillside getaways – an area of distinctive villages itself.

RICHMOND AND CREMORNE

Just beyond Yarra Park with its famous sporting grounds is Richmond Hill, a high point favoured by the wealthy from the earliest days of European settlement for its picturesque views of the Dandenong Ranges. It is still a desirable location, but Richmond's place in the popular imagination remains as a working class struggle town thanks to the noxious trades and industry established here by the 1860s, using the river to shift their waste. Workers lived close by, in row upon row of tiny workers cottages built on tiny narrow streets. It would have been a sharp contrast to the mansions with spacious gardens at ritzy Richmond Hill. And while the timber gold-rush era cottages were replaced by brick land boom era terraces in the 1880s, the subdivisions on the flat remained small and the buildings slummy well into the 20th century.

Richmond's signage dazzles day and night.

Depression in the 1890s and the 1930s made this poor community even poorer so it's no surprise that petty crime, bookmaking, money laundering, drug dealing and sly grog selling all flourished in the absence of jobs. Some of Richmond's more notorious sons include gangster Squizzy Taylor (*see* box, p. 148), bookmaker John Wren, criminal Dennis Allen and drug trafficker Van Tuong Nguyen.

Working class Richmond, however, was also the birthplace of some of Australia's most loved household items: Redhead's matches, Wertheim pianos, Pelaco shirts, Slade knitwear, Nuttlex spread and Rosella tomato sauce. The Dimmey's department store clock on Swan Street is a local landmark, and Cremorne in particular is a great suburb to walk for its historic product signage.

Postwar immigration along with the state government's slum reclamation program transformed the suburb in the mid 20th century. Tower blocks were built off Victoria Street, and walk-up flats on the site of John Wren's old pony race track by the Yarra River. Next door, GTV-9 took over from the Wertheim piano factory. Industry began moving out as the end of the 20th century approached, and Melburnians began to discover the charm of inner city living – whether in industrial chic converted warehouses or new luxury apartments.

Richmond's Nylex Clock has been a local icon since 1961, now replicated on posters, T-shirts, bags and in songs too.

Nylex clock

The same designer of skipping girl Little Audrey (*see* p. 151) on Victoria Street was also behind the Nylex Clock, erected atop the Richmond malting silos in 1961. For almost 50 years, the Nylex clock has reminded Melburnians of the time and the temperature during their daily commute – helping sell hundreds of thousands of plastic garden hoses and making Australia's largest plastics manufacturer a household name in the process. Though Paul Kelly immortalised the 'clock on the silo' in his 1987 song 'Leaps and Bounds', the clock was inoperative by the end of the 1990s. A heritage listing in 2003 led to restoration in 2005, but when Nylex was placed into receivership in 2007 the clock was switched off. Urban explorers switched the clock back on in January 2015, after which electricity company AGL agreed to power the sign themselves.

GTV-9

Though Melbourne television station Channel Nine has been located at Docklands since 2011, for most Melburnians Bendigo Street is still where TV is made.

But before it was GTV-9 it was the Wertheim piano factory. Here, at 22 Bendigo Street, was Australia's largest piano factory. Hugo Wertheim desired a prestigious factory, and spent upwards of £25,000 to achieve it. The investment was considered so significant that Prime Minister Alfred Deakin laid the foundation stone himself in 1908, and at its peak the factory produced 2000 pianos a year. Wertheim was famous for all-purpose upright pianos built specifically for Australian conditions, and counted Dame Nellie Melba among its clients. The 1930s Depression affected the fortunes of the business, but worse was competition from radio, and the Melbourne factory closed in 1935. The company continues today, manufacturing pianos in China and Korea.

Following the closure of the piano factory, Heinz processed tinned foods at the site before GTV-9 took over the premises in 1956. The following year, Graham Kennedy launched the

THE BLACK WIDOW OF RICHMOND

ONLY FIVE women were hanged in Victoria during the period of capital punishment. Three were for infanticide, but Martha Needle – the Black Widow of Richmond – was a cold blooded murderer and a rare female serial killer. Having grown up in a violent and abusive household, she was known to be mentally unstable from a young age. She married Harry Needle in 1880 when she was just 17, and by 1885 they had three daughters. But by 1890, Martha Needle had poisoned them all. In the process she collected hundreds of pounds in insurance money – spending almost all of it on an elaborate family grave in the Kew cemetery, which she visited often. Doctors were baffled by the sudden, mysterious deaths.

Newly single, Martha took in lodgers. She began an affair with one, Otto Juncken, in 1893, but their marriage was prevented by his brothers, Louis and Herman. The following year, Louis mysteriously died. While settling his brother's affairs, Herman Juncken became ill after eating with Martha on three separate occasions. Suspecting poisoning, his doctor took a sample of his vomit and found it contained arsenic.

Herman and the doctor informed the police and a trap was set when Herman again went for lunch at Martha's. After being served a cup of tea, Herman summoned detectives by actually blowing a whistle. This time, Martha had been determined to finish the job: the cup of tea was found to contain enough arsenic to kill five people. She was charged with attempted murder. Otto Juncken maintained that she can't have known what she was doing.

The bodies of her husband, daughters and Louis Juncken were all exhumed and found to contain fatal levels of arsenic. Martha maintained her innocence, but was found guilty after a three-day trial and sentenced to death. When asked for her last words she replied, 'I have nothing to say.' She was executed at 8am on 22 October 1894. (On 15 July 1920, Martha's nephew was hanged for poisoning his wife with strychnine.)

First a piano factory, then GTV-9's studio, now apartments.

nightly variety show *In Melbourne Tonight*, which also featured Bert Newton. Both became household names and Australian TV legends.

Variety shows and infomercials made up a large chunk of the line-up in the 1950s and 1960s; one of the longest-running variety shows, *Hey Hey it's Saturday*, launched in 1971 and ran almost continuously until 1999. Talk shows emerged in the 1970s, and the network embarked on its most expensive drama production, *The Sullivans* (*see* box, p. 202), in 1976, which was entirely shot in Melbourne. Other dramas shot locally include *Stingers* and *Underbelly*. Richmond was also the location for Richard Lowenstein's cult film *Dogs in Space*, about the Melbourne post-punk Little Band Scene of the late 1970s. The film is fairly plotless, following the day-to-day lives of a group of characters led by Michael Hutchence's Sam as they party in the shadow of the Pelaco sign.

The station has been owned by cinema chains, radio stations, newspapers, production houses and television manufacturers but most notable among them has been the Packers' Australian Consolidated Press, who sold the network to Alan Bond in the 1980s and bought it

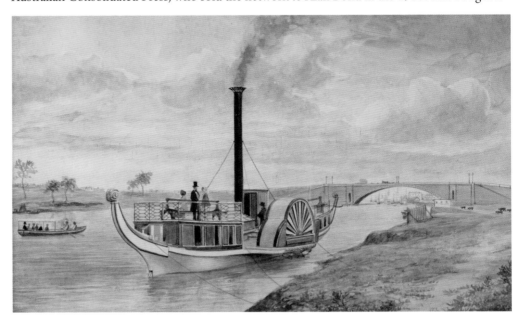

En route to Cremorne Gardens from Princes Bridge, 1855.

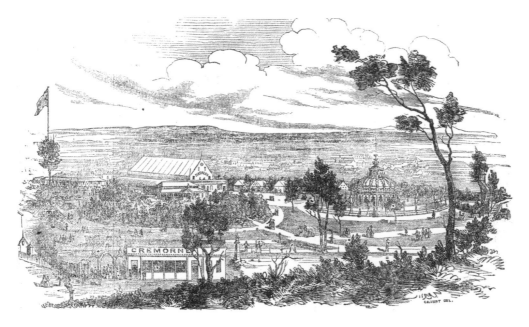

Charles Somerton's 1862 lithograph of the Cremorne Gardens. The rotunda at right, prefabricated in New York, housed the orchestra and was surrounded by an open-air dance floor.

back for a steal a year later. The transaction made the Packers millions; as Kerry Packer once said, 'You only get one Alan Bond in your life and I've had mine.'

Cremorne pleasure gardens

If you've ever wondered where Cremorne got its name, you'll find the answer in a pleasure garden. Established in 1853 by James Ellis, who had earlier managed the Cremorne Gardens in London, they were immediately successful but heavily criticised for the availability of liquor and sex. Public perception of the place changed, however, when theatre entrepreneur George Coppin acquired the gardens in 1856. Visitors caught gondolas from Princes Wharf, alighting on the north bank of the Yarra near Cremorne Street to promenade around the gardens, marvel at the cyclorama and menagerie of exotic animals (including six camels he later sold to Burke and Wills), play skittles, watch tightrope performances and dance the night away before the evening fireworks. In 1858, thousands came to watch William Dean lift off on the first balloon flight in Australia and in 1859, the Melbourne and Suburban Railway Company even built a train line to the gardens.

The Cremorne Gardens were Coppin's pure indulgence; he failed to make any money from them, and was declared bankrupt in 1863. The gardens were closed and the land sold – first for an asylum but later bought and subdivided by Thomas Bent (*see* box, p. 224), who left his name in the suburb's Bent Street. A small park on Cremorne Street is all that remains of the former pleasure gardens. A true entrepreneur, Coppin rose like a phoenix to establish a seaside resort at Sorrento (*see* p. 232).

Stately Willsmere, for decades Melbourne's main asylum and now luxury apartments.

HAWTHORN AND KEW

Hawthorn and Kew are among the wealthiest, leafiest and least industrial suburbs in the city. Starting out as a farming community, Hawthorn grew up from a little township at the corner of Church Street and Burwood Road. In 1860, a bridge across the Yarra at Bridge Road connected the little town to the rest of the city and encouraged land speculation, as did the extension of the railway from Burnley to Hawthorn in 1861. From there, Hawthorn and Kew developed as commuter suburbs; as the *South Burke Standard* newspaper noted in 1863, the residents were 'that class who get their breakfasts, went away into town, and returned at night for their suppers'.

But Hawthorn and Kew really are a product of the 1880s land boom. Ornate churches and elite schools were built, as well as many opulent residences. A working class also moved in to single-fronted cottages on low-lying subdivisions around the suburb's brickworks. Look around at Hawthorn's distinctive clay bricks – known as pinks, blacks and brown.

Neighbouring Kew followed a similar pattern of development. Deriving its name from its proximity to Richmond – just like the suburbs of the same names in London – Kew's rich soils and access to the river made it ideal for agriculture. A bridge at Johnston Street opened in 1858 and another at Victoria Street in 1884, and it was the large mansions of Studley Park that dominated the area then and continue to define the suburb today. The vast Yarra Bend Park in a bend in the river has been a hidden-away location for numerous asylums since the 1850s.

Today, Hawthorn and Kew are widely considered to be the prettiest suburbs of Melbourne. The elevation affords expansive views across the river to the city and out towards the ranges, and together they comprise the densest concentration of independent schools in the country, many housed in the former grand mansions of the city's 19th century elite.

Studley Park mansions

Elegant mansions clustered early on Studley Park Road, including Studley Hall, the Villa Alba and Burke Hall, now part of Xavier College and formerly the home of bookmaker John Wren. But it is Raheen – still a seat of local power – that best typifies the extravagance and opulence of the boom mansions of the 1880s with its wide driveway leading to a grand two-storey red brick Italianate style mansion, prominent tower, arcaded loggia, ballroom, library, internal courtyard with fountain and fernery, rear service wing, private stabling, carriage house and even its own dairy. Substantial lawns and gardens still surround, though originally it maintained a river frontage.

Formerly Knowsley, Raheen was built in 1870 for Carlton Brewery owner Edward Latham (later father-in-law of WL Baillieu, whose mines at Broken Hill and the La Trobe Valley are just two among many big ventures). Barrister and solicitor Henry Wrixon owned it for a time until the Catholic Church bought it in 1917 to use as the official residence of its archbishops, the most famous of which is Daniel Mannix (*see* p. 77). Raheen was bought in 1981 by recycling magnate Richard Pratt, and he and his wife Jeanne restored the property and added a new wing by renowned Australian architect Glenn Murcutt in 1992. It's a private residence today, but some of the grandeur of Raheen is visible from the street, inaccessible though it may be behind solid brick fences and tall hedges – just as it was intended to be.

Behind the austere Italianate facade of the Villa Alba on Walmer Street is an unusual ornamental painted interior. For much of the 20th century the Villa Alba was a home for nurses, during which time much of the mansion's decorations – which cover walls, cornices and ceilings in many rooms – was painted over. Created by the Paterson Brothers interior decorators in 1883, these fine art murals – depicting scenes from literature as well as Sydney Harbour and Edinburgh – were at the pinnacle of fashion in land boom era Melbourne. The practice was not confined to private homes; you can also see painted decoration in public buildings such as the Government House ballroom, the Royal Exhibition Building and the

The majestic 1870 Raheen, showing the 1992 Glenn Murcutt wing.

Advertisement for the select neighbourhood of Grace Park Estate showing the Kew Railway Line.

Gothic Bank. The Villa Alba is open to the public on the first Sunday afternoon of every month.

Grace Park Estate

Taking its name from Grace Park House – built in 1858 on a 95-acre property bordered by Power Street to the west, Barkers Road to the north, Glenferrie Road to the east and Burwood Road to the south – Grace Park Estate was subdivided for housing in 1884. It is one of the finest estate developments in the city; its history visible in a walk along its streets.

Grace Park House is still there, on Chrystobel Crescent at the centre of the subdivision. But looking at the estate on a map, you can see it is incomplete – several of its crescents were never finished due to the onset of the 1890s depression. And the curiously curved LE Bray Reserve that cuts through the estate? That wasn't part of the original subdivision plan: it conceals the Kew Railway Line, built through the estate in 1887 with stations at Barkers Road and Wellington Street. The line operated until 1952, mostly without success. Numerous extensions were proposed to increase the prospect of the line's viability – including to Doncaster, still a dream of many Melburnians – though none ever got up. The Glenferrie Oval was built on the uncompleted section of the estate in 1905; the rare Art Deco grandstand added in 1937.

Studley Park Boathouse

Now within the enormous Yarra Bend Park, Studley Park is important for its indigenous flora as well as the oldest continuously operating boathouse in Australia. Built in 1863, the Studley Park Boathouse remains a popular spot for recreation today. It had been popular for walking and exploring since the 1830s, but it was the Burns family's decidedly Victorian boathouse that really transformed the park in the second half of the 19th century – and inspired the establishment of tea gardens on the Yarra at Fairfield and also on the Maribyrnong River at Avondale Heights, where picnickers could dip their feet in the water, hire a boat for a paddle, or take tea in spacious rooms overlooking the river and bush.

Around the bend from the boathouse, Deep Rock was a popular swimming hole for locals, complete with its own club and lifesavers until the 1940s. In 1918, more than 70,000 people watched freestyle swimming inventor Alick Wickham make a world record dive of 62 metres from a tower atop the riverside cliffs during a charity fundraiser. When he hit the water, he allegedly lost consciousness – and his bathers.

During the 1930s, Studley Park was given a boost by an unemployment relief project to create a scenic Yarra Boulevard at Kew, replicating the one in Burnley and providing an almost continuous scenic riverside drive from the city to Alphington. Unfortunately cars also empowered drivers to travel further afield, and the Studley Park Boathouse declined in popularity – becoming a rooming house and a boat workshop until restoration in the 1990s gave it a new lease of life.

The 1863 Studley Park Boathouse, still a favourite place for picnickers and bushwalkers, a boat ride or simply a chardonnay in quiet bushy surrounds.

Yarra Bend asylums

The Yarra Bend Park, where Merri Creek converges and the river doubles back on itself, is a remote and isolated place. Perfect for institutions that require separation from the public.

The Yarra Bend Golf Course – on the north bank of the Yarra – is the site of the city's first lunatic asylum, as mental health facilities were then known. It opened in 1848, providing an institution for those considered insane, who were previously imprisoned. By 1856 the facility was declared unsuitable, and a new asylum was built further east on the south bank of the river in 1872, despite the sustained objections from Kew residents. The new Kew Asylum was one of the grandest buildings ever constructed in Melbourne, and even today remains a landmark structure for miles around.

Built to comfortably accommodate 600, by 1873 – just one year after opening – it was seriously overcrowded with more than 1000 patients. An 1876 inquiry revealed inadequate water supplies, shortages of basic amenities and brutality by staff. Recovery rates for patients hovered around a low 25 per cent. The Cottages for Idiots, which became Kew Cottages, opened in 1887 to provide accommodation for children and young adults with intellectual disabilities. Efforts to reduce the stigma associated with mental hospitals resulted in several

This doctored image showing Edward de Lacy Evans in male and female attire was used to promote his appearances as the mysterious man-woman.

EDWARD DE LACY EVANS

EDWARD DE Lacy Evans arrived in Victoria in 1856 amid a cloud of speculation. He had boarded the *Ocean Monarch* 'dressed in a green merino dress and sealskin coat' and wore it and a men's shirt and trousers for the entire voyage. He is alleged to have formed sexual attachments with several women on board, but was he a man or a woman? After arriving in Melbourne he married Mary Delahunty at St Francis's Church on Elizabeth Street, but by 1862 Mary had remarried – claiming that her first marriage was not legal because Evans was a woman. Edward married again in 1868 – to the sister of a friend of his former wife. She had a baby in 1877, and though Edward was listed on the birth certificate he was not the father.

In 1879, a curious incident occurred. Admitted to the Bendigo Hospital for being 'dangerous to others', he refused to take a bath as prescribed and he escaped. He was arrested at his home the following day and committed again but still refused to bathe. Six weeks later he was transferred to Kew Lunatic Asylum where it was discovered he had been born physiologically female. The case caused a sensation in local and international newspapers, as well as significant distress to Edward as he was made to wear female clothes until his release. Outed, he made several appearances as a curiosity: male impersonator and mysterious man-woman. He died in 1901, remembered only in passing in Joseph Furphy's classic Australian novel *Such is Life*.

name changes – the Hospital for the Insane in 1903, the Mental Hospital in 1930, the Willsmere Psychiatric Hospital in 1960 – but these could not hide the neglect of the facility and its patients. Willsmere was finally closed in 1988 and has since been redeveloped into luxury heritage apartments.

From psychiatric facility to luxury apartments, WIllsmere has been home to numerous famous residents.

The original Yarra Bend Asylum, however, was not discontinued. The buildings in the north of the park were still in use in 1925, and in 1927 were converted into a hospital for the treatment of infectious diseases. This too closed in 1951, and was refurbished into Victoria's first women's only prison, Fairlea, which operated from 1956 until the Kennett government's prison privatisation program closed it in 1996.

Tom Wills (*see* box, p. 74) spent time here, and so too did Walter Richardson – father of the Australian author Henry Handel Richardson and the subject of her trilogy *Fortunes of Richard Mahoney*, a fictional retelling of her father's decline from a brain disease and its effects on her family.

Outer Circle Railway

Everyone complains about the bottleneck of traffic on the Chandler Highway bridge over the Yarra at Kew. It's no wonder: it's an old single lane bridge and never actually built for cars.

The Outer Circle Railway is nostalgic for many because it was a dream that provided a cross-town shortcut. Sure we have the 1970s city loop encircling the Hoddle Grid, but most of us travel into and out of the city on radial lines from the suburbs. But it has not always been that way.

First proposed in 1867, the outer circle was originally envisaged to carry Gippsland line trains north-west from Oakleigh and in to Spencer Street. At the time of the Gippsland line's construction in the 1870s, the government did not own the train tracks between South Yarra and Princes Bridge – and so sought an alternative route into the city. The government's 1878 takeover of the railway solved that problem; as did the viaducts built between Princes Bridge, Flinders Street and Spencer Street in 1891.

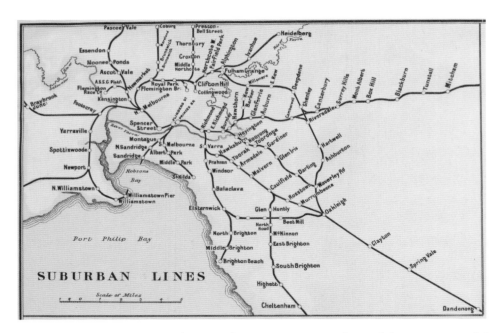

SUBURBAN LINES

Map of Melbourne railways in 1893. Note the inner circle had not yet been built.

Developer-politicians including James Munro ensured the line was included in the 1882 and 1884 *Railway Construction Acts*, and bought vast tracts of land adjoining it, subdividing and auctioning more new estates. But by the time it opened in 1890, the land boom had already peaked. Sales were slow, passengers were few, and the train sprinted through open country for much of its 20-kilometre journey. Sections began to close in 1893 and the line was closed completely in 1897. The line, however, wasn't a total failure. The Camberwell to Ashburton section reopened in 1898, electrified and extended to Alamein in 1924. Where it passes through Glen Iris, it is bounded by Prosper Parade on one side and Welfare Parade on the other – place names that reference the mood at the time of their construction.(From 1900, the Deepdene Dasher steam train connected Riversdale with Deepdene, but it was not electrified and closed in 1926.)

An inner circle line had earlier been formed in 1888, first by joining Royal Park on the Upfield Line with Merri on the Whittlesea Line (now South Morang) via Park Street, North Fitzroy. A branch line served Fitzroy via Edinburgh Gardens. The Heidelberg (now Hurstbridge) Line also used the same track, the driver awkwardly having to change ends at Clifton Hill until a new line was built from Princes Bridge to Clifton Hill in 1901 – thereby completing the loop. From then on, Hurstbridge and South Morang train lines ran directly via Hoddle Street, negating the need for the old line. The Victorian Railways experimented with running 'roundabouts' and by 1906 were running an hourly service from Princes Bridge to North Fitzroy via Clifton Hill. The line was electrified in 1921 and passenger services extended to North Carlton on weekdays and Royal Park on weekends for zoo day-trippers. A new station was opened at Rushall in 1927, but its roundabout route and competition from more direct trams meant the route was not viable, and it was eventually closed in 1948. North Carlton Station survives as a community centre on the Capital City Trail, one of the city's most trafficked bicycle routes.

CAMBERWELL AND CANTERBURY

Camberwell takes its name from the pub that once stood at its distinctive six-ways junction – just like the London suburb. Decidedly rural until the 1860s, it became progressively more urbanised as wealthy settlers moved in to establish estates with gardens, vineyards and even a few cows. The suburb was connected by train in 1882 and its population had almost quadrupled by 1892.

But Camberwell's genteel character is distinctly 1920s – a result of another land boom that followed the electrification of tram lines. All the while, Camberwell residents maintained

THE MINOGUES

RAISED IN Surrey Hills, educated at Camberwell High, stars of such quintessential Melbourne shows as *The Sullivans*, *Neighbours*, *The Henderson Kids* and *Young Talent Time*, the Minogue sisters Kylie and Dannii pretty well epitomise eastern suburban success.

It was the younger Dannii who landed a role on Johnny Young's variety show, *Young Talent Time*. Kylie auditioned too, but it wasn't to be. Her two-year turn as mechanic Charlene Mitchell on *Neighbours* changed all that; and her 1986 on-screen wedding to sometimes real-life boyfriend Jason Donovan is one of the most-watched Australian TV episodes of all time and an iconic moment in Australian TV history. The following year she landed a record deal with Mushroom Records after performing 'The Loco-motion' at a Fitzroy Football Club fundraiser. The song became the highest-selling Australian single of the 1980s and before long she was working with UK hit factory Stock, Aitken and Waterman pumping out hit after hit. In the early 1990s Kylie was romantically linked with Michael Hutchence and in 1995 dueted with Nick Cave on 'Where the Wild Roses

Grow', both major turning points in her career. The 2000 release of her seventh album was something of a comeback with the lead single, 'Spinning Around', topping the charts in both the UK and the US. To date, she has sold more than 10 million albums.

Dannii, meanwhile, left *Young Talent Time* to join Sydney soapie *Home & Away* and later to launch her own clothing range, known as Dannii. She released her first album, also called *Dannii*, with Mushroom Records in 1990 and soon after headed to the UK to continue recording and pursue TV hosting.

THE SULLIVANS

PAINSTAKINGLY RESEARCHED and meticulously set designed, *The Sullivans* followed the lives of Camberwell's Sullivan family, their friends, neighbours and associates during World War II. *The Sullivans* won numerous Logies during its eight-year run and remains one of the most popular Australia dramas ever produced. Many of its actors went on to enjoy successful careers, including Mel Gibson, Kerry Armstrong, Kylie and Dannii Minogue, Michael Caton and Sam Neill.

The Retreat Hotel in Abbotsford was the setting for The Sullivans' Great Southern.

spacious gardens on large blocks, and the council planted street trees and preserved creek verges and public parks. So perfect was this suburban life that Camberwell, along with neighbouring Box Hill, voted to close its pubs – even the one for which it was named. It later became a milk bar.

Camberwell residents successfully fought off development in the suburb until the 21st century – even storming council meetings and getting themselves elected to council to overturn a development proposal that ultimately cost the City of Camberwell $25 million in damages. More recently the satirist Barry Humphries (aka Dame Edna *see* box, p. 182) – who has made a living lampooning Camberwell privilege – campaigned against development around Camberwell Railway Station.

Ye olde Maling Road, 2015.

Maling Road

In neighbouring Canterbury is the storybook historic shopping strip Maling Road, built in the shadow of the Canterbury Railway Station. Its Victorian- and Edwardian-era shops – now taken up with antique stores, cafes and boutiques – are a miraculously preserved streetscape replete with full street-side verandahs.

BOX HILL, BALWYN, BULLEEN AND BEYOND

Occupied by squatters in the late 1830s, then part of Henry Elgar's 1841 Special Survey, the little town of Box Hill emerged on the road between Melbourne and Lilydale during the 1850s. Small farm holders moved in during the 1860s, orchardists in the 1870s, and the extension of the train to Box Hill in 1882 opened up the land for speculation. 1930s Box Hill replete with orchards is brought to life by Emily Bitto in her 2015 Stella-prize winning book *The Strays*.

Brickworks sprang up across Balwyn, Bulleen and Box Hill, though they've long since been converted into the pretty parks that these suburbs are known for. Beckett Park, with its observation tower and century-old Maranoa native gardens, crowns the highest point in inner Melbourne – and was for many years the site of Empire Day bonfires. Balwyn and Bulleen flourished after World War I and are among Melbourne's most prestigious estate suburbs. Balwyn takes its name from 1850s *Age* editor Andrew Murray's vineyard, now the site of Fintona Girls School. From 1889 until 1896 Box Hill was the departure point for the country's first electric tram, which travelled to a lookout on Doncaster Hill along a route now called Tram Road.

A large community of tee-totalling Methodists congregated in Box Hill in the 1910s and by 1920 the anti-liquor campaigner EW Greenwood had been elected to state parliament on a platform to close pubs in Camberwell and Box Hill, including its namesake White Horse Hotel.

There is very little industry and few business districts in this area, which serves to give it a unique history. Australian glam rock band Skyhooks may have mocked Balwyn for its brick veneer prisons in their 1974 hit 'Balwyn Calling', but the suburb is unmoving in its suburban exclusiveness – perhaps even more so than Toorak and South Yarra.

Box Hill, on the other hand, took a different trajectory. By the 1970s it had a population

THE WHITE HORSE

THOUGH IT'S famous for being a dry area, the City of Whitehorse and its main road actually take their names from a pub established in 1853. After it was closed in 1920 it became a boarding house before being demolished in 1933. The 25 centimetre statue of a white horse that adorned the pub was saved and presented to the council, and is now preserved inside the Box Hill Town Hall.

of almost 50,000 – up from 20,000 just twenty years earlier. The local council actively consolidated its trading status against the popularity of shopping centres at Doncaster and Ringwood by putting the train station underground and expanding a market over it. They also welcomed a large number of new Asian residents, primarily from China and Vietnam, who have transformed the area into a popular foodie destination for a range of Asian cuisines.

The Heidelberg School

Tom Roberts' 1890 painting Shearing the Rams, *a masterwork of the Heidelberg school and inspiration for Australian artists since.*

Though the term 'Heidelberg School' has come to mean Australian Impressionism at its broadest, the term finds its genesis in a small group of *en plein air* painters who sought to capture the Australian bush, and in particular the Australian sun. While the name comes from one of their camps at Heidelberg, they painted all the way up the Yarra Valley, from Bulleen to Yarra Glen. Tom Roberts, Arthur Streeton, Frederick McCubbin and Charles Conder are just the best known painters among the group of artists who painted the Australian landscape as it really is, providing generations of Australians since with their quintessential impression of an Australian bush landscape.

In the 1970s, their work took on renewed importance as Australian filmmakers used it for inspiration. Most notable among them is Peter Weir's film of Joan Lindsay's novel *Picnic at Hanging Rock*; Ken Hannam's *Sunday Too Far Away*, which even recreates Tom Roberts' *Shearing the Rams*; *The Chant of Jimmie Blacksmith*, *The Getting of Wisdom* and *My Brilliant Career*.

Heide

The next major movement in Australian art after the Heidelberg School was the establishment of Heide by John and Sunday Reed. John Reed had been a successful lawyer and Sunday Reed a member of the prestigious Baillieu family. After moving in to a little farmhouse on the Yarra in 1934, they built up an impressive modernist library and progressive group of friends including the artists Sidney Nolan, Albert Tucker and Joy Hester.

Though Joy Hester and Albert Tucker married in 1941, Sunday Reed famously said that artists shouldn't have wives – and it's the complicated personal lives of the Heide Circle that has given it such mystique. The 1940s were a busy and exciting time at Heide. Albert Tucker painted his *Images of Modern Evil*, Sidney Nolan painted his iconic Ned Kelly series in the dining room at Heide, and John Reed became the publisher of *Angry Penguins*, a surrealist literary magazine that was the target of a literary hoax in 1943 when early modernist poets James McAuley and Harold Stewart faked a body of work to humiliate the magazine's 22-year-old editor, Max Harris. It was an unsettling experience for the young editor, though he maintained his belief in the work's quality and it is still referenced today.

The circle began to fall apart in 1947. Joy Hester was diagnosed with Hodgkin's Lymphoma that year, and decided to give her son Sweeney to the Reeds to raise so she could move to Sydney to be with the artist Gray Smith. Sunday Reed's long affair with Sidney Nolan also came to an end that year, and he left a valuable collection of artworks behind, though Sunday Reed eventually returned them all. In 1963, the Reeds commissioned Heide II – 'a gallery to be lived in'. The state government bought the Heide farmhouse and Heide II in 1980 for the creation of a public art gallery and park. John Reed died on 5 December 1981, and Sunday Reed ten days later.

TOP The house where it all began.
ABOVE Heide III showing Emily Floyd's work out front.

Montsalvat

The working artists' colony of Montsalvat was established by artist and architect Justus Jörgensen in 1934, and comprises numerous cottages, studios, galleries, a hall and chapel. It was named for the castle of the knights of the Holy Grail of German mythology, and is a great place to see some materials reclaimed from buildings demolished by Whelan the Wrecker. The limestone windows of the Great Hall are from the Royal Insurance Building that once stood at

The Great Hall at Montsalvat.

414 Collins Street, and the hall's cast-iron spiral staircase was reclaimed from Bourke Street's Bijou Theatre.

Jörgensen's friends and students constructed many of the buildings themselves and by hand, and Montsalvat's unique construction – particularly the use of rammed earth building techniques (knowledge allegedly acquired by reading Pliny at the State Library of Victoria) – later inspired local architects to build mud-brick houses and use reclaimed materials in their buildings.

Numerous artists have been associated with Montsalvat over the years, most notably the painters Albert Tucker and Clifton Pugh and the stained glass artist Leonard French. After 80 years it is still a place of enduring creativity, and living onsite today are numerous painters, gold- and silver-smiths, glass artists, couturiers, luthiers and a shakuhachi flute maker.

THE DANDENONGS

Thirty-five kilometres from the CBD, the Dandenong Ranges are the eastern lip and the highest points of the great basin that Melbourne occupies, and from Mt Dandenong on a clear day you can see as far as Mt Macedon to the north and the You Yangs in the west. The ranges' highest points are 633 metres at Mt Dandenong, and 628 metres at Mt Corhanwarrabul. Viewed from Fitzroy – say the Naked in the Sky rooftop atop the old Moran and Cato building on Brunswick Street – their thickly wooded mountain ash slopes form a prominent, bluish periphery.

To European eyes the Dandenongs were first a source of timber but by the 1870s it was a popular destination for day-trippers. Vast tracts of wet and dry sclerophyll forest were preserved in the 1880s and now form the Dandenong Ranges National Park. They have always been prone to bushfire, and were badly affected in 1983, 1997 and 2009.

The train to Upper Ferntree Gully was completed in 1889, but it was the Village Settlement Scheme that arose out of the 1890s depression that created the ranges' first townships at Ferny Creek, Monbulk and Mooroolbark. From 1900, a narrow-gauge railway connected right through to Gembrook and gave orchardists access to city markets for the first time. A tourism industry had emerged by the 1920s, with day-trippers enjoying picnics in tea gardens, bushwalking, scenic drives and bicycle riding. Wealthier visitors built their own country houses and gardens or simple weekenders. The quirky Cuckoo smorgasboard restaurant, with its Bavarian floor show, dates to 1958; before that it was refreshments kiosk The Quamby, which had operated since 1914.

Melbourne's population growth after World War II pushed at the foothills of the Dandenongs, and new residents were soon making the long commute to work in the city. The maturing of several major gardens that are open to the public, and the reopening of the Puffing Billy steam train line in 1998 has regenerated tourism, with visitors coming to explore the scenic drives, walks and rides, picnic spots, gardens, restaurants and cafes and spectacular views from Mt Dandenong itself.

Puffing Billy

Constructed in 1900 to help establish towns beyond the ranges, the narrow-gauge Gembrook railway initially ran 30 kilometres from Upper Ferntree Gully to Gembrook. Timber fellers,

Postcard showing perennial children's favourite Puffing Billy.

nurseries and fruit and vegetable growers despatched lumber, cut flowers, saplings and produce, while day-trippers also ventured into the ranges on special weekend excursion trains. Many of the locomotives in use on the line were built at the Newport Workshops and previously used at the West Melbourne Gas Works.

Though the line carried more than 50,000 passengers in 1920–21, its days were numbered in the 1930s when the Victorian Railways' own buses and trucks began competing for passengers and freight. When the line was cut by a landslide just east of Belgrave in 1953, the Victorian Railways closed it. But after a series of farewell rides in the 1954–55 summer attracted tens of thousands of children, the volunteer Puffing Billy Preservation Society was formed and trains continued to steam into Belgrave from Upper Ferntree Gully. When that section of the line was electrified in 1958 as part of the extension of Melbourne's suburban railway system, the Puffing Billy Preservation Society prepared to reopen the rest of the line to Gembrook. Enlisting the help of

HORATIO JONES HOUSE

HORATIO JONES' house, in a hidden valley in Tecoma, is an extraordinary example of ingenuity and tenacity in the face of hardship. Born in 1871, Horatio Jones was an inventor and engineer. He showed his self-adjusting windmill in the juvenile category of the 1888 Centennial Exhibition and lived a fairly comfortable life in South Yarra, working in the metal trades as an engineer.

Engaged to be married to an American woman at the outbreak of World War I, Horatio enlisted – aged 43 – and landed at Gallipoli in August 1915. He was discharged the following year due to rheumatic fever. Returning home he discovered his father had died, both his sisters' fiances had been killed in the war and his mother died shortly thereafter. Worried he would not live much longer, he persuaded his fiancee to end their engagement, move back to America and forget about him.

Grief-stricken, sick and impoverished, Horatio sold the family home and bought a small property on Ferny Creek at Tecoma. Using hand-made tools, by 1920 Horatio had built a two-storey house out of saplings, fencing wire, kerosine tins, river rocks and whatever other materials he could salvage. His sisters occupied the top floor, Horatio the bottom, and the trio re-created the family home with blackwood four-poster beds, a piano, dining settings, oriental screens, Persian rugs and regular soirees for friends. They kept fruit trees and a veggie patch, bees and an exotic garden, and legend has it that Horatio even entertained poet CJ Dennis and artist Arthur Streeton in his own backyard studio. A water-wheel on the creek generated electricity, and provided the lighting to the outdoor dunny.

the Citizen Military Force, they built a new section of track to bypass the landslide and, decade by decade, the line was progressively reopened all the way to Gembrook by 1998.

Today Puffing Billy is a major tourist attraction, and Melburnian children well know the thrill of hanging their legs out the open windows, passing through Sherbrooke Forest and over the trestle bridge, which is classified by the National Trust, and picnicking at Emerald Lake. The line's restoration and ongoing preservation is a great example of Melburnians' dedication to their history and the railway's importance to the essence of the Dandenong Ranges.

The Alfred Nicholas Memorial Gardens, open to the public and resplendent all year round.

Burnham Beeches

This magnificent Art Moderne mansion and gardens was the country house of Alfred Nicholas, one of the founding partners of pharmaceutical giant Nicholas International.

Starting out with a kerosene tin and some kitchen utensils, George Nicholas, Alfred's pharmacist brother, set out to replicate aspirin when the Australian government suspended the patents for it following the outbreak of World War I. By the end of 1915, the brothers were in business – and thinking ahead to register their product as Aspro in Australia. It was a slow start, but by the end of the 1920s the Nicholas' had expanded into Europe and Asia – and made hundreds of thousands of pounds worth of philanthropic gestures to Melbourne organisations.

Burnham Beeches at Sassafras is a testament to the family's wealth as well as Alfred's love of gardening. Designed by Harry Norris (Nicholas Building, Majorca Building, GJ Coles Building, Mitchell House, Curtin House), the three-storey Burnham Beeches – completed in 1933 – is light and airy, commanding yet controlled. Zig-zags decorate the wrought-iron balustrades and moulded relief panels on the exterior feature koalas and possums. Inside was an electric pipe organ and a private theatrette 'with the latest talkie equipment'.

It was surrounded by a small farm, extensive gardens with orchid houses, artificial waterfalls and was even flood-lit at night.

Following Alfred's death in 1937, the house became a research facility for the company and in 1965 the gardens were gifted to the local shire. It has changed hands a couple of times since – most recently in 2010 when it was purchased by a consortium including Vue de Monde restaurateur Shannon Bennett, who is in the process of refurbishing the property into a sustainable resort with hotel, spa, wellness centre, villas, café, bakery and restaurant.

TOP Stairs leading to Burnham Beeches from the Alfred Nicholas Memorial Gardens. BOTTOM The Cuckoo, formerly The Quamby, restaurant and tea rooms in operation since 1914.

Mt Dandenong

Atop Mt Dandenong is a lookout across the vast urban sprawl of the city, best viewed at night when the city glitters like Christmas lights. The peak's elevation made it the logical site in the 1950s for the city's television transmission towers, and ever since they have broadcast radio and television into the city's homes.

The cool climate and shady aspect of the Dandenongs has resulted in the establishment of numerous nationally significant gardens. The Mt Dandenong Arboretum of mixed conifers and deciduous trees was the first public garden established here in 1928. Next was the William Rickett's Sanctuary, an unusual sculptural garden begun in 1934 and featuring the Aboriginal-inspired artwork of local potter William Ricketts.

Set out on more than 100 acres, the National Rhododendron Gardens is the largest. Surrounded by thick mountain ash – the tallest flowering plant in the world – there are more than 15,000 rhododendrons here, as well as 12,000 azaleas, 3000 camellias and many thousands of other flowering bulbs and plants. The RJ Hamer Arboretum, established

following bushfires in the 1970s, features massed plantings of European and Asian trees in a broader forest of Australian eucalypts and acacias.

 The adjacent peak, Mt Corhanwarrabul, is the site of Australia's worst air disaster. The Kyeema Track leads to the memorial cairn that remembers the 18 passengers and crew killed in 1938 when the Kyeema DC-2 hit the mountain after massively overshooting Essendon Airport in heavy fog.

The sprawling city from Mt Dandenong at night.

Chapter Eight

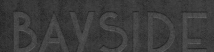

ST KILDA

ELWOOD

BRIGHTON

SANDRINGHAM, BLACK ROCK AND BEAUMARIS

THE MORNINGTON PENINSULA

MELBOURNE'S BAYSIDE SUBURBS from St Kilda to Sorrento

have always been a seaside playground and a secluded getaway for the city's rich and famous. Some of the city's most distinctive icons are located by the bay, such as St Kilda's Luna Park and Brighton's famous bathing boxes (*see* p. 225), all bathed in the salty seaside air.

Further afield is the Mornington Peninsula, where Melburnians keep beach houses for weekend getaways and longer summer sojourns, and increasingly spend their retirement years.

ST KILDA

St Kilda was Melbourne's first seaside leisure town. It takes its name from the yacht *Lady of St Kilda* moored offshore in 1841. Located at the north-east corner of Port Phillip, St Kilda Beach is well protected from ocean swells, and with its high ground above the beach offering a cool breeze in summer, it's easy to understand why St Kilda very quickly became fashionable for wealthy European settlers.

Bathing boxes, tents and cottages were recorded at the St Kilda foreshore 'for bathing season' as early as the 1840s, substantial homes were built on the suburb's gentle rises throughout that decade and the next, and with the arrival of the railway in 1857 came increasing numbers of day-trippers and sea bathers.

Public bathing, however, was strictly prohibited during daylight hours in the 1850s, and would remain confined to privately run sea baths until the 1910s. First, they came for Captain Kenney's Bathing Ship – the *Nancy* – which he had scuttled off the St Kilda Pier in 1854 for bathers to frolic upon. By the 1860s numerous baths had

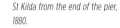

St Kilda from the end of the pier, 1880.

BELOW *Captain Kenney's bathing ship, the Nancy.* **OPPOSITE** *Brighton's famous bathing boxes with the city looming behind.* **PREVIOUS PAGES** *(left and right) Bathing boxes have been a fixture of Port Phillip Bay since the 1840s.*

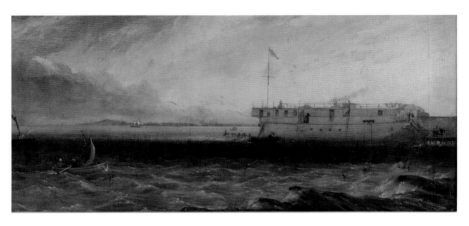

been constructed along the foreshore, either exclusively for men or with separate sections for women, each with stairs for discrete entry to the water. Business quickly boomed off the back of the popular belief in the health benefits of the sea and sun, despite the dangers: the sight of men bathing naked and predatory marine creatures.

But it was the coming of cable trams in 1888 that really transformed St Kilda into the pleasure zone we still know today, bringing day trippers first from the city, South Yarra and the inner north, and by the 1910s from as far afield as Malvern and Kew.

Four different Palais have been built here since 1913, with the 1927 Palais Theatre still standing today. Though it's under threat of demolition it has some high profile supporters, including Rolling Stone Mick Jagger. The St Moritz Ice Rink was built in the precinct in 1939, but was lost to fire in 1982.

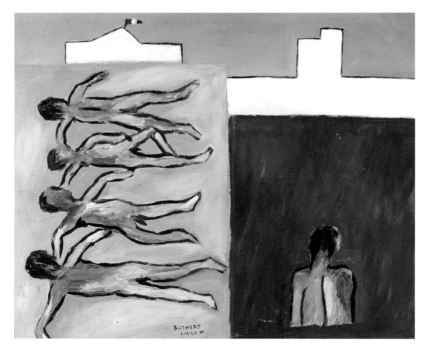

But the suburb's character changed during the Depression of the 1930s, largely due to the Melbourne City Council's effort to clean up notorious Little Lon (*see* p. 46); St Kilda's many parks provided a cheaper alternative to rented rooms. The outbreak of WWII in 1939 and the subsequent influx of Australian and American service personnel further increased the popularity of St Kilda's entertainments.

The 1930s and 1940s was also the period during which Melbourne's Jewish community began to congregate in the area. Acland Street's European cafes and cake shops, most notably Monarch Cakes and the now defunct Cafe Scheherezade, were the community's heart for decades, though the centre of Jewish life in Melbourne has now moved east to Caulfield.

Heide (see p. 204) artists Sidney Nolan and Albert Tucker both depicted St Kilda in their work. Nolan depicted the joie de vivre of St Kilda Beach in his series The Bathers (above), while Tucker recorded its seedier side in his series Images of Modern Evil.

From the late 1960s, St Kilda became known for its bohemian culture, with its artists, musicians and sub-cultures, including punks and gays, but today St Kilda is a backpacker

Luna Park's scenic railway is the oldest continuously operating roller coaster in the world – and it's made of wood.

paradise. Irish, English, Spanish, German and Scandinavian accents ring out across the bars and pubs of Fitzroy Street but St Kilda Beach is still the place's main drawcard – whether for swimming, sunbathing, kitesurfing, playing beach volleyball or taking in the sights while walking, cycling or skating along the foreshore paths that now extend all the way to Beaumaris. A visit to the European cake shops of Acland Street is a quintessential Melbourne experience, as is a snap of Luna Park.

St Kilda Pavilion

Looking down the pier to the St Kilda Pavilion and the breakwater.

A landmark destination from the time it was built in 1903 was James Charles Morell's Edwardian St Kilda Pavilion. Appearing almost marooned at the end of the pier, the pavilion has been colloquially named after the families who operated it. Probably no one remembers it as Parer's Pavilion, but many will know it as Kerby's Kiosk, when it was at the centre of many Melburnians' memories of icy poles on hot summer's days or a windy wedding photo shoot. After it was destroyed in an arson attack in 2003, it was rebuilt to its original 1903 plans, even using materials that survived the fire, including the cast-iron roof and weather vane. The breakwater at the end of the pier shelters St Kilda Harbour as well as the little penguin colony that still calls this place home, located now on the edge of a metropolis.

St Kilda Sea Baths

The 1920s saw a significant change in Melbourne's moral values. Having formed in the 1910s, the Open Sea Bathers League challenged and finally overturned prohibitions on open sea

St Kilda Sea Baths before they fell into disrepair.

bathing (legalised in 1917), Sunday bathing (1922) and mixed bathing (1927). Going to the beach as we know it today was born. Open sea bathing also sounded the death knell for sea baths, as local councils began erecting changing pavilions along the foreshore. These too have had their time, though the St Kilda Beach bathing pavilion survives today as the iconic Donovan's restaurant.

The St Kilda Sea Baths we know today were built in 1929. Featuring Moorish domed towers, Spanish Mission parapets, Islamic fretwork screens and arcades facing the shore, these baths – the largest in Victoria – confidently anticipated a busy future, containing 756 lockers for men and 572 lockers for women. Opening in 1931, their time had already passed and they quickly fell into disrepair and were partially demolished in the 1950s. Later, several notorious nightclubs operated inside the pavilions, but violence, vandalism and fire saw them closed in the 1980s and the baths in their entirety in 1993. Refurbished in the following decade with only the facade remaining, the

CARLO CATANI

PERHAPS THE person who changed St Kilda more than any other is the Italian-born engineer Carlo Catani, who master-planned the famous leisure precinct once compared to Coney Island and still largely intact today. Catani received his civil engineering diploma from the Technical Institute of Florence but left Italy in search of work. He arrived in Melbourne in 1876 and joined the Department of Lands and Survey as a draftsman.

By 1892, Catani was working for the Public Works Department, in charge of draining the Koo-Wee-Rup swamp, and then widening the Yarra River upstream from Princes Bridge. By mid-1897, he was planting elms, oaks and poplars along the bank and the newly formed Alexandra Avenue. Further afield, he drained swamps and built levees along the Murray River.

In 1906, Catani was contracted to prepare a master plan for the beautification of the St Kilda foreshore all the way to Point Ormond. He reclaimed the foreshore and established gardens, promenades and space. The first St Kilda Sea Baths were built in 1910, followed in 1912 by the famous Luna Park with its garish face and scenic railway.

Catani personally designed the gardens named in his honour, and you can see a bronze bust of him at the base of the clock tower that also bears his name. His vision allowed Melburnians orderly, leisurely access to the waterfront from St Kilda to Point Ormond; today the Bay Trail extends his continuous public foreshore all the way to Beaumaris.

St Kilda Sea Baths today contain Australia's only indoor heated sea baths.

The Tolarno Hotel

Mirka Mora mural at Flinders Street Station.

Opened in 1966, this Melbourne institution was the third restaurant of art patrons Georges and Mirka Mora, who came to Melbourne from France in 1951. Both had escaped the Holocaust – Georges in the French Resistance, Mirka hiding with her family in the forests of France. In Melbourne they cultivated an artistic and bohemian clientele at their restaurants Cafe Mirka on Collins Street (opened in 1954, it was one of the first al fresco cafes and hosted the first exhibition of works by Heide artist Joy Hester) and Balzac in Wellington Parade, East Melbourne (the first restaurant in Melbourne to hold a 10pm licence). Firmly ensconced in Melbourne's artistic and culinary life by the mid 1960s, the Moras expanded their vision at Tolarno with a gallery and artist studio for Mirka alongside the restaurant. The Tolarno Galleries exhibited the work of artists including Charles Blackman, Sidney Nolan and Howard Arkley alongside Mirka's own bold works featuring recurring motifs of angels, children, dogs and cats. Her work is collected at Heide Museum of Modern Art (*see* p. 204).

The Moras sold Tolarno in 1969 to Leon Massoni of Cafe Florentino and relocated Tolarno Galleries to River Street in South Yarra, where they continued to support contemporary art, most notably supporting the development of Juan Davila. The couple separated in 1971 and Georges died in 1992. Mirka is today a national treasure, and their son Tiriel well known to many as jaded journo Martin di Stasio in TVs *Frontline* and small-time lawyer Dennis Denuto in the movie *The Castle*.

(*see* p. 204)

FROM ST KILDA TO KINGS CROSS

ST KILDA HAS long been known for its music scene. It was in the Crystal Ballroom at The George Hotel on Fitzroy Street that Nick Cave and his entourage got their start in the early 1980s, as well as Hunters and Collectors and the Models. The Prince of Wales is a similarly legendary live music venue, and the Greyhound, host to drag shows for fifteen years, has been an anchor of the south side gay community. Paul Kelly's 'From St Kilda to Kings Cross', with its line 'I'd give you all of Sydney Harbour (all that land, all that water) for that one sweet promenade,' conveys the locals' love for the place, and you'll hear St Kilda referenced in myriad other songs by local artists.

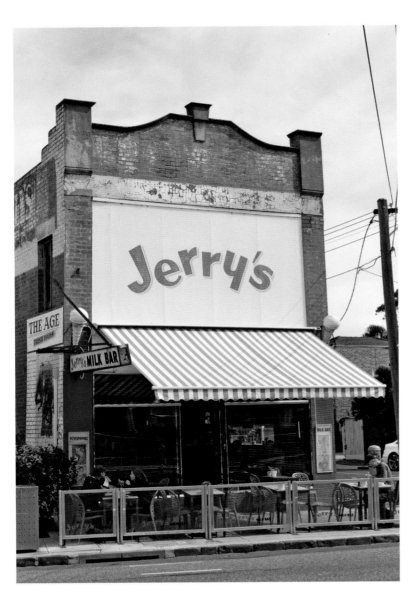

Jerry's taps in to the nostalgia for Australian milk bars of the 20th century.

ELWOOD

Elwood's proximity to the beach makes it one of the city's most sought-after suburbs. Village life goes off here, tucked away as it is from transport thoroughfares. And it is this relative isolation that has given the suburb its prestige. Elwood's charming street names derive from the sea (Beach Avenue, Spray Street, Wave Street, Tide Street and Foam Street) and British writers (Shakespeare Grove, Dickens Street, Milton Street, Wordsworth Street, Byron Street, Keats Street, Tennyson Street, Ruskin Street and Shelley Street).

Initially planned around the Elster Creek – now the Elwood Canal – the Elwood area was for generations a gathering place of Aboriginal people attracted to the swampland rich in water fowl and the coast abundant in cockles. At the Little Red Bluff at Point Ormond they would cook shellfish and burn signal fires, but by the 1900s the Little Red Bluff was reduced to a little grassy knoll after it was levelled and used to create a seawall and reclaim swampland. The first radio-telegraph between a ship and an Australian telegraph station took place here in 1901, and even today a little tower on the bluff is used for signalling.

Point Ormond Quarantine Station

Point Ormond has a sad history as Victoria's first quarantine station. In 1840 the immigrant ship *Glen Huntley* entered Port Phillip with its fever flag flying, indicating illness aboard. The ship had been overcrowded: though it had been specially built to carry immigrant workers to Australia and was on its maiden voyage, the ship's master saw profit before people. Of the 157 who boarded at Argyleshire in England, ten had died at sea. A quarantine station of canvas tents was hastily erected at Point Ormond, then quite remote from the town of Melbourne, and the unfortunate emigrants disembarked a week after arriving in Port Phillip.

The passengers were divided into sick and healthy camps: 39 in the former and 108 in the latter, though all were emaciated and fatigued from the long journey. To make matters worse, the camps were exposed to cold and wet weather. Three more would die before all passengers were given the okay to travel to Melbourne in early June – six weeks after arriving.

The quarantine station was closed in the 1850s and its operations moved to Point Nepean (*see* p. 234). The graves of the three who died remained enclosed in a white picket fence on the bluff until 1898, when coastal erosion threatened the site. The graves were reopened in the presence of government representatives and even the daughter of one of the victims, and the bodies reinterred at St Kilda Cemetery.

Elwood Canal

Elwood Canal is the defining feature of this suburb, and has shaped Elwood's development. The swamp once collected the run-off from 40 square kilometres of south-east Melbourne, and was also the site of noxious trades and St Kilda's night soil dump until the 1900s. By 1888, the stench from the swamp was widely regarded to be a nuisance, and 60 men were employed to construct a concrete canal from Glenhuntly Road to Elwood Beach to a design by Carlo Catani (*see* box, p. 218). A dredge imported from San Francisco pumped sand and clay from the Elwood foreshore mixed with water into the swamp, and by 1905 the St Kilda council reported that the swamp had been

The Elwood Canal has been a swampy creek, polluted drain, and now much-loved waterside promenade.

The Sun *newspaper's annual beach girl competition, held at St Kilda Beach, 1958.*

drained. Engineer John Monash (*see* box, p. 98) was concurrently engaged to construct several bridges across the canal. The one at St Kilda Street is the oldest surviving concrete girder bridge in Victoria, possibly Australia. You can also spot mooring rings along the canal's walls, originally intended for tying up pleasure boats.

The first land sales of the reclaimed swamp took place in 1908, and was progressively sold off until the 1920s, which explains the predominantly art deco houses and apartment buildings. Though the canal now blooms with water plants and scenic walking tracks, it was long maligned as a glut for pollution, known to locals as Plague Canal. Local parents banned their children from the canal following an outbreak of polio in 1937, and the local school even closed from June to September that year as a result. Illegal rubbish dumping in the canal was an annoyance to locals for years.

Storms and high tides over the years have shown the canal is ineffective at preventing flooding, and additional drains have been built to reduce the flow of water during heavy rain. Still the canal drew negative attention – when a young Prince Charles swam at Elwood in 1970 he described the water as 'diluted sewage'.

COUNTDOWN

PRODUCED AT the ABC's Ripponlea studios, *Countdown* is one of the most culturally significant programs to have screened on Australian TV. With Ian 'Molly' Meldrum as host, *Countdown* gave new life to the Australian music scene in the 1970s and 1980s and also popularised the use of music videos. Crucially, it kickstarted the careers of local acts such as AC/DC, INXS and Kylie Minogue (*see* box, p. 201).

BRIGHTON

Brighton's first non-Indigenous landholder was Henry Dendy (*see* box), who in 1840 purchased 5120 acres at Port Phillip for £1 per acre, site unseen. He arrived in February 1841 to claim his land, *imaginatively* named Waterville, bounded by the coast on the west, North Road, East Boundary Road and South Road. The township was surveyed with distinctive crescents and renamed Brighton in May 1841. Unfortunately Dendy's future was more tragic than bright; despite being named Waterville his land holding did not actually contain any water. Sales were slow and his plan quickly failed. The family of his agent, Jonathan Binns Were, who negotiated Dendy's purchase of the land, bought it all back from him. Dendy died poor, a mine rail driver at Walhalla in Victoria's east. The Weres went on to become one of the richest families in Melbourne.

Bathers at Brighton Beach, 1967.

Today Brighton is home to some of the city's wealthiest citizens and most lavish houses. But Brighton's most influential resident was unquestionably the land boomer Thomas Bent (*see* box, p. 224). He was mayor of the council nine times, and anchored every major project in the suburb between 1874 and 1894, bringing trams and duplicating the railway.

HENRY DENDY'S SPECIAL SURVEY

IN AUGUST 1840 the British Government allowed the purchase of land anywhere in the Port Phillip District for just £1 per acre for eight square miles. It was a price significantly below value, and eight special surveys were taken up in 1841. Just three of them were in present-day Melbourne: Henry Dendy's at Brighton, Frederick Unwin's at Templestowe and Henry Elgar's at Box Hill. Their sale had been restricted by Governor Gipps to no closer than eight kilometres from a township and with only a limited waterfront. All three of these surveys have affected the alignment of Melbourne's roads because their boundaries did not all conform to Robert Hoddle's survey lines. In Brighton, North, South and Boundary Roads all point to the original boundaries of Henry Dendy's Special Survey. As the *Sydney Gazette* noted in 1841, 'Those gentleman who have been fortunate enough to obtain special surveys in our province have had ample reason to be thankful ... Verily the time for speculating in land has not yet gone by.'

THOMAS BENT

BORN IN New South Wales, young Tommy Bent came to Melbourne with his parents in 1849. After attending school in Fitzroy he became a market gardener in East Brighton, but gave it up in 1861, aged 21, to become a rate collector for the Brighton Town Council. By 1871 he was a member of parliament, and in 1881 was made commissioner for works and railways. Bent certainly believed in progress and Victoria's destiny as a prosperous colony, and privately and in parliament he worked tirelessly on directing and sustaining the land boom – using public money to underwrite expansion. As commissioner for railways he introduced the *Octopus Act*, promising lines to all electorates in order to gain parliamentary support, and inflating the value of his own investments with the duplication of the Brighton line in 1882. Uncovered, it was a scandal that led to the defeat of the government at the 1883 elections.

Miraculously Bent retained his seat and quietly retired to the backbench where he concentrated on his property developments. He was a key player in the land boom of the 1880s, and he would have been bankrupted by the crash if he had not transferred many of his assets to his wife. He lost his seat at the 1894 election, his fate sealed when the *Age* published letters Bent had written when he was railways minister in 1881, offering MPs railways in their electorate in exchange for their votes.

He and his wife and daughters then moved to the south-west town of Port Fairy, where he took up dairy farming – though still with one eye on politics. By 1900 he was back as the member for Brighton ... and up to his old tricks too – approving a tram from St Kilda to Brighton that led right past his properties.

Despite his dodgy behaviour, Bent became premier in 1904 at the age of 66, when Premier Irvine quit to go into federal politics. He was knighted in 1908 and died in 1909. His statue, erected by public subscription in 1913, became a well-known landmark for locals and travellers on the Nepean Highway at Bay Street, where it was yearly decorated with a cap and scarf in the colours of the premiership-winning footy team, other times defaced by a bucket of paint. In the 1970s it was moved to a less prominent location to accommodate the widening of the highway, its landmark status diminished.

Eighty-two bathing boxes line Brighton Beach, but the local council may allow more in the coming years.

Bathing boxes

Brighton has long been a beachy getaway for Melburnians. But no one played beach volleyball in boardies or budgie smugglers in the old days. Here at Brighton, bathers preserved their modesty within the suburb's famous brightly coloured bathing boxes, which are believed to date as far back as 1862 and were first located at the water's edge at Bay Street. By the turn of the century there were more than 100 bathing boxes lining Brighton's beaches. During the 1930s Depression, the local council's capital works program to relieve unemployment relocated all bathing boxes to Dendy Street Beach. Eighty-two remain today, a favourite subject for photographers – particularly when viewed from Green Point with the Melbourne city skyline in the background.

Each box is the same size and build, and Bayside City Council's heritage overlay restricts alterations. So all the bathing boxes retain their Victorian-era architecture, including timber frames, weatherboard sidings and corrugated iron roofs – and without such modern conveniences as electricity or running water. If you're in the market for one you better move to Brighton as they can only be purchased by residents paying local council rates. How much? Approximately $200,000 plus annual rates of around $500 – and no, you're not allowed to reside in one.

Several sea baths were erected along Brighton's beaches in the 19th century. The 1881 Middle Brighton Municipal Baths are the only remaining caged open water sea baths in Australia – albeit rebuilt and repaired after being wrecked by storms on three occasions. The Art Moderne buildings we know today were built by local architects Oakley and Parkes. The hardy Brighton Icebergers swim here every day of the year.

BRIGHTON TORNADO

THE BRIGHTON Tornado is the strongest storm ever recorded in Melbourne. Late in the afternoon of a sultry day in February 1918, three tornadoes struck Brighton Beach and moved across the suburb, killing three people and injuring six. A church was destroyed, roofs torn off houses and hotels, and the 1861 Brighton Baths were wrecked.

Inspired by Frank Lloyd Wright's Guggenheim Museum in New York, architects Oakley and Parkes built the Brighton Civic Centre in 1959.

The scuttled wreck of the HMVS Cerberus, Victoria's first warship and an early prototype of the modern battleship.

SANDRINGHAM, BLACK ROCK AND BEAUMARIS

Named Gipsy Village when the first lots were sold between 1852 and 1854, and re-named Sandringham in 1887, Sandringham was very slow to grow, with the post office opening, closing and re-opening between 1868–73. Black Rock was similarly sleepy during this period, though Beaumaris was sold in a frenzy with the promise that a railway was imminent and that a canal would be built. That never eventuated, and Beaumaris was only barely skirted by the railway in 1881.

Meantime, the Beaumaris Tram Company made do with a horse-drawn tram service from Sandringham to Cheltenham through Beaumaris, and an electric tram ran from Sandringham to Black Rock until 1936.

Picnic Point with its sea baths and Half Moon Bay with its red cliffs made this area a popular beach resort in the 19th century, and today the Bay Trail traces the coastline and its Aboriginal, maritime and leisure history.

J7

J-class submarines in Sydney in 1919.

The Sandringham Yacht Club boasts a number of Sydney to Hobart yacht race winners, and for almost 90 years an 83-metre British World War I submarine known as *J7* has acted as a breakwater, its rusting hull providing moored boats with protection from Port Phillip. These days a 326-berth marina overshadows the 1700-tonne sunken hulk.

Built in 1916–17 the J-class was a seven submarine class developed by the British Royal Navy. Though not as fast as surface vessels as their architects had hoped, the submarines still sank a U-boat and damaged two battleships, with the loss of just one to friendly shelling. Following the war, the six surviving submarines were gifted to the Royal Australian Navy to protect the Pacific. When they arrived in Australia, they were in poor condition. Refitted in the early 1920s at the Commonwealth Naval Dockyards in

Sydney, all were scuttled around Melbourne in 1926: *J7* to form the breakwater at Sandringham and another at Swan Island off Queenscliff; the rest in the ships' graveyard at Barwon Heads.

HMVS Cerberus

A more famous scuttle at nearby Half Moon Bay, with its picturesque oxidised orange cliff, is the iron-clad *HMVS Cerberus*, commissioned by the newly formed Victorian Navy in 1866 and scuttled here in 1926. The need for defence? An entirely unfounded but much feared Russian invasion. The gold coursing through the city must also have felt like an obvious target for seaborne raiders.

An illustration of the HMVS Cerberus in training with the HMVS Nelson in Port Phillip Bay, circa 1860s.

Jointly funded by the British and Victorian governments, *Cerberus* was built in England to a radical new design. She was the first British warship to be powered solely by steam and to feature rotating gun turrets mounted on a central superstructure – the first of all modern battleships. *Cerberus* became a flagship of the Victorian Navy and was eventually withdrawn from service in 1924. The Cerberus naval base at Flinders is a testament to her service.

Black Rock House

Black Rock takes its name from Charles Hotson Ebden's unusual seaside getaway, Black Rock House, built in 1856. Its high castellated walls were constructed from bluestone cut from nearby Quiet Corner, and surround the large timber house. Edben made a mint being among the first overlanders from New South Wales, but he had also earlier attended the first land sale in Melbourne in 1837. He was three times elected to the Legislative Council of New South Wales – before Victoria became a separate colony. In 1851 he became auditor-general in the first Victorian government, representing the seat of Brighton. He was also a dandy, and a member of the Melbourne Club who indulged his talent for epigrams: his flippant remark that he feared he was becoming 'disgustingly rich' became as famous as his wealth. Upon his death his estate was valued at more than £100,000, and over 100 carriages followed his hearse to the Melbourne General Cemetery.

Friends of Black Rock House conduct free tours.

*Charle Hotson Ebden's Black
Rock House.*

*The Beaumaris Cliffs, inspiration for
generations of artists.*

Beaumaris Cliffs

The Beaumaris Cliffs, from Charman Road to Table Rock, are of international importance as a site for marine and terrestrial fossils. Ricketts Point is a popular beach area at the end of the marine sanctuary that extends all the way to Black Rock.

At Ricketts Point, there is a monument commemorating the Heidelberg School artists (*see* p. 204). Tom Roberts, Frederick McCubbin and Louis Abrahams spent the summer of 1886–87 working from a rented house in Mentone to paint *en plain air* (out of doors) at the Beaumaris Cliffs. Roberts wrote of seeing the young apprentice lithographer Arthur Streeton who was 'standing out on wet rocks painting' and his work 'was full of light and air'. They, and later Charles Conder, all painted memorable pictures of the shores of Beaumaris and Mentone, capturing the distinctive bright light of bay.

CHADSTONE

OPENED IN October 1960, Chadstone Shopping Centre is the largest drive-in shopping centre in the Southern Hemisphere. The first was actually the Heidelberg Mall, built by the Housing Commission in 1956 for the Olympics, but Chadstone was always intended to be something else altogether.

Chadstone was the brainchild of Kenneth Myer, who had been researching US retail trends in the 1950s following the growth in car ownership. It was the beginning of the move away from Melbourne's traditional high street shopping. At first Chadstone was an open-air mall with a Myer at one end and a Dickins supermarket at the other. Melbourne's climate, however, wasn't particularly conducive to open-air shopping, so in 1967 a fibreglass roof was added.

But it was the sale to the Gandel Group in the 1980s that really created Chaddy, as it's known to locals. Since the 1990s the centre has been expanded considerably, and is now composed of more than 500 stores, cinemas and other entertainments, food courts and restaurants spread over more than 200,000 square metres, all serviced by approximately 10,000 car spaces. Soon, there'll be a hotel on site too. Chadstone reportedly turns over $1.4 billion a year – the highest turnover of any shopping centre in Australia – and is visited by more than 20 million people annually.

BACKGROUND *Chadstone Shopping Centre was not even a dream in 1930, when this aerial photograph was taken. The curved road at centre is Waverley Road, left of that is East Malvern Station, then still connected to the Outer Circle Railway line. In the distance is the farmland that would become Chadstone Shopping Centre and the vast suburbia it serves.*

The view from Arthurs Seat.

THE MORNINGTON PENINSULA

Stretching from suburban Frankston to Point Nepean at the entrance to Port Phillip Bay, the Mornington Peninsula is the city's seaside holiday playground. The coastline on turbulent Bass Strait, however, has also claimed numerous lives over the years, including a sitting prime minister.

John Murray in the *Lady Nelson* was the first to make it through the notorious Port Phillip Heads in February 1802, followed by Matthew Flinders just ten weeks later – then on his voyage to chart the Australian coastline. Both remarked on the pleasing, fertile appearance of the land. Fearing French ambitions in the area, the British government organised to get in first and despatched David Collins to establish a colony at Port Phillip. They abandoned the settlement (*see* p. 232) after just three months, but the escaped convict William Buckley (*see* box, p. 233) lived on with the Aboriginal people for 32 years.

Fears of French ambitions never really went away, and so New South Wales Governor Ralph Darling authorised a second attempt at settlement in 1826. This too got the location wrong (near present-day Corinella in Western Port Bay) and the settlement was abandoned in 1828, the departing settlers burning the buildings down so they couldn't be used by escaped convicts. (French Island, in the middle of Western Port Bay, is today the largest intact pre-contact environment in the Port Phillip region.)

The establishment of Melbourne on the Yarra River in the 1830s eventually brought squatters to the peninsula, as well as lime-burners, loggers, fishermen and quarrymen. They were

The Point Nepean Highway, still a track in this Rose Series photograph from the 1940s. The Dromana Pier is visible in the distance.

later joined by farmers, orchardists and winemakers. The quarantine station was established at Point Nepean (*see* p. 234) in 1852 and by the 1870s the well-to-do were building summer residences all along the peninsula, which they reached either via comfortable bay steamer from Queenscliff – then the seaside getaway for Melbourne's elite – or the rough track that has since become the Nepean Highway. Early residents include artist and diarist Georgiana McCrae, businessman and politician WL Baillieu, and *Picnic at Hanging Rock* author Joan Lindsay.

Generations of Melburnians have made a home away from home on the peninsula during summer.

The fort at Point Nepean was built in 1886. Train lines were built to Mornington and Stony Point in 1889 and to Red Hill in 1921, all to service the peninsula's local industries as part of the Village Settlement Scheme. But it was the motor car that really made the peninsula what it is today. By WWII, middle-class Melburnians had chosen Rosebud for their summer getaway, at first erecting tents and later towing caravans and even bringing the TV with them to make a home away from home. Often they'd return to the same campsite every year. All the cars killed the Mornington and Red Hill railways, and today the Mornington Peninsula is now part of suburban Melbourne and dotted with distinctive Mornington Peninsula style architecture of light, bright houses and casual spaciousness.

Homes on the Mornington Peninsula nestle among the scrub.

Entrance to the Dromana drive-in with its replica Star Wars fighter jet.

Dromana drive-in

Dromana's drive-in cinema is one of only three remaining in Melbourne – there are also drive-ins at Coburg and Dandenong – but it's the only one that has continuously operated since it opened in 1961. Just as Kenneth Myer pioneered the development of US-style suburban shopping centres, Hoyts brought drive-in cinemas from the US to Australia in the early 1950s. The first opened in suburban Burwood in 1954 and was so popular it caused traffic jams on Burwood Highway. Soon enough, drive-ins were popping up all over the suburbs. Built to accommodate 485 cars, Dromana's drive-in now contains three screens playing movies six nights a week, each serviced by the kitschy American Shel's Diner at the centre of the parking lot. Dromana's original 1961 screen is still in use.

Sorrento

Lieutenant-Governor David Collins, circa 1800s.

At present-day Sorrento is the site of the first attempted British settlement in Port Phillip. Sailing from Portsmouth, England in April 1803 Lieutenant-Governor David Collins led the *HMS Calcutta* and the merchant vessel *Ocean* on the six-month voyage. Collins had with him 300 convicts and more than 100 soldiers and free settlers. They arrived in October 1803 and set up at Sullivan Bay near present-day Sorrento, just inside the bay. It was defensively well sited and secured Bass Strait as a trading route – it took days off the journey to Sydney, and the area was also well known for its abundant whales and seals.

After a week of observations, soldiers and convicts made camp on the beach, with Collins, the Reverend Knopwood, the surveyor James Tuckey and free settlers on the gentle rise behind. But without ready access to water it would only ever be short-lived. Tuckey explored the bay, noting the profusion of wildflowers but failed to find a suitable water source. So to make do they fashioned a water system by burying their casks with the outer chamber filled with sand and grasses. They'd hoped this method would filter the water but it was still too salty. Sickness ensued, pessimism and insubordination grew and the colony's days were numbered.

Still, life went on. A baby was born and baptised, Knopwood set his hens on eggs and smoked well into the night, convicts cleared land and went cray fishing, settlers sewed cucumbers and melons, soldiers got drunk (each was allowed half a pint of spirits per day), and everyone watched the ocean for a friendly Union Jack or an enemy tricolour. Among the few children who played on the beach was a young John Pascoe Fawkner.

WILLIAM BUCKLEY

HEARING OF the plans to abandon the Sorrento settlement, numerous convicts escaped, including one named William Buckley. While most convicts were captured or returned, Buckley remained at large for 32 years – eventually presenting himself to Batman's party at Indented Head on the Bellarine Peninsula in 1835.

Born in 1780, Buckley had fought in the Netherlands against Napoleon before he was transported in 1800 for receiving stolen goods. He was a giant of a man – over two metres tall – and described by a contemporary as 'a tall, ungainly man ... he had a shaggy head of black hair, a low forehead with overhanging eyebrows nearly concealing his small eyes, a short snub nose, a face very much marked by smallpox, and was just such a man as one would suppose fit to commit burglary or murder'.

Buckley survived by joining a group of Watha wurrung people after a long solo walk around Port Phillip Bay. He was befriended by some Aboriginal women after he had taken a spear marking an Aboriginal grave to use as a walking stick. Legend has it that they recognised the spear as belonging to a relative recently deceased, and believed Buckley to be his ghost. Over the next 32 years he learned their language and their way of life, and claimed to have had two wives and a daughter.

Encountering John Batman's party at Indented Head in July 1835, Buckley at first said he was a shipwrecked soldier but later revealed his true identity and in September was granted a pardon by Governor George Arthur in Van Diemen's Land. Buckley then became an interpreter and in 1836 accompanied Joseph Gellibrand on a trip west of Melbourne, during which Gellibrand recounted: 'when we arrived at the spot I witnessed one of the most pleasing and affecting sights. There were three men, five women and about twelve children. Buckley had dismounted and they were all clinging around him and tears of joy and delight running down their cheeks.'

But Buckley quickly became disenchanted with white society and colonisation. He moved to Van Diemen's Land in 1837, where he married in 1840. In 1852, John Morgan helped him write *Life and Adventures of William Buckley*, which historians today regard as a sometimes limited but compelling and accurate account of pre-contact Aboriginal life. William Buckley died in 1856.

The expression 'You've got Buckley's' refers to Buckley's chances of survival away from the settlement. Over time, the expression gained emphasis as it evolved into 'You've got two chances: Buckley's and none', also referencing the old Melbourne department store Buckley & Nunn.

The Queenscliff–Sorrento ferry, providing daily connections for more than 150 years.

By 6 November, however, Collins had resolved to abandon the settlement. The captain of the merchant vessel *Ocean* refused to sail though so a volunteer crew of convicts set out for Port Jackson in a rowboat. It took them three days to clear the Heads, at which point the *Ocean* took them aboard – the captain having changed his mind. They returned on 12 December with approval to leave Port Phillip for Van Diemen's Land.

During the 1860s, entrepreneur George Coppin – bankrupted after the failure of his Cremorne Gardens (*see* p. 193) – devised a plan to develop Sorrento into a holiday resort. By 1870, he had built the Sorrento Pier and begun running daily steamers from Melbourne to Queenscliff and Sorrento. He also built the Continental Hotel, swimming baths and, together with other investors, inaugurated a steam tramway service in 1890 to carry visitors from the Sorrento Pier to the back beach, where they could admire the wild natural scenery and ocean. From here, Portsea also emerged – still to this day the most exclusive of Melbourne's seaside resort towns.

Point Nepean quarantine station and fort

At the very tip of the Mornington Peninsula, Point Nepean National Park is the site of the southern tip of the Heads that guard Port Phillip Bay and has overseen numerous shipwrecks and lives lost. It is also the location of a 19th century fort and quarantine station.

The treacherous Port Phillip Heads.

Though the Heads are more than three kilometres apart, the navigable channel through them is just 300 metres wide. The surrounding reefs mean these are treacherous waters. Certainly you should never go in alone, though that's exactly what Prime Minister Harold Holt did at Cheviot Beach in 1967, never to return. His body was never found, which continues to fuel conspiracy theories. The Harold Holt Memorial Swimming Centre in Glen Iris commemorates his death.

A sanatorium was gazetted for Point Nepean in 1852 to take over from the quarantine station at Point Ormond (*see* p. 221) at Elwood, which had long been deemed unsuitable. But before it was even built it had a plague ship upon it when the *Ticonderoga* anchored offshore on

3 November 1852. It had departed Liverpool with 714 passengers and 48 crew, but 100 had died from typhus and scarlet fever en route. Another 70 died at Point Nepean, the little quarantine station then made up of tents and some wattle-and-daub huts.

By 1855 the station could accommodate 450 people in canvas tents and about 40 people on iron beds in a hospital. Building continued apace throughout the 1850s, and numerous passengers were quarantined with typhus, scarlet fever and smallpox. There were more deaths, but by the 1860s the station was also used for the convalescence of hundreds of children from the industrial school at Princes Bridge who were suffering from eye infections. While there, some of the children contracted measles, scarlet fever and other diseases.

Arguments were made that the station's low occupancy meant that quarantine was unnecessary, and the value of the quarantine station's land was regularly noted. But the government continued to invest in quarantine facilities, such as bathing and disinfecting complexes in the late 1890s, and isolation huts to combat the global influenza pandemic that followed the First World War. During the 1910s it was used as a summer school for Victorian teachers, and in 1998 the buildings were used to temporarily house refugees from the war in Kosovo.

Fort Nepean was progressively built at the Point from the late 1870s. This, along with the batteries at Queenscliff, Swan Island and South Channel Island, and mines in the channel itself, replaced Fort Gellibrand (*see* p. 169) as Melbourne's first line of defence. Though Melbourne was never really in anyone's sights, the value of the city's gold, the Crimean War and Russia's naval activity were all sources of concern. And so by 1888 Point Nepean and Fort Queenscliff were both equipped in the event of attack. Though that never transpired, the first Allied shots in both world wars were fired from Point Nepean, far from the originating conflicts. On 5 August 1914, the German steamer *Pfalz* was fired upon as it was about to proceed through the Heads, just as war had been declared. The crew was arrested and the ship refitted as an Allied transport for the duration of the war. On 4 September 1939, a warning shot was fired at a boat attempting to enter the Heads without identifying itself. It turned out to be a Tasmanian freighter!

REFERENCES

Annear, Robyn, *A City Lost and Found*, Text Publishing, Melbourne, 2005.

Annear, Robyn, *Bearbrass*, Text Publishing, Melbourne, 2005.

Annear, Robyn, *Nothing but Gold*, Text Publishing, Melbourne, 1999.

Australian Bureau of Statistics, *2011 Australian Census QuickStats*, www.census.gov.au, multiple entries accessed September 2014–March 2015.

Australian Dictionary of Biography, National Centre of Biography, Australian National University, published first in hardcopy 1966, www.adb.anu.edu.au, multiple entries accessed December 2014–March 2015.

Barnard, Jill, *People's Playground: a History of the Albert Park*, Chandos Publishing, Melbourne, 1996.

Barrett, Bernard, *The Inner Suburbs: The evolution of an industrial area*, Melbourne University Press, Melbourne, 1971.

Bate, Weston, *A History of Brighton*, 2nd ed., Melbourne University Press, Melbourne, 1983.

Bate, Weston, *Essential But Unplanned: The Story of Melbourne's Lanes*, State Library of Victoria, Melbourne, 1994.

Blainey, Geoffrey, *A Game of Our Own: The Origins of Australian Football*, Black Inc., Melbourne, 2003.

Blainey, Geoffrey, *Camberwell*, Lothian, Melbourne, 1980.

Blake, Louise, "Rescuing the Regent Theatre", *Provenance: The Journal of Public Record Office Victoria*, no. 11, Public Record Office Victoria, Melbourne, 2012. www.prov.vic.gov.au/publications/provenance/provenance2005/rescuing-the-regent-theatre#sthash.ColHQ7JN.dpuf, accessed January 2015.

Blazey, Peter, *Bolte: A Political Biography*, Jacaranda Press, Melbourne, 1972.

Boyce, James, *1835: The Founding of Melbourne and the Conquest of Australia*, Black Inc., Melbourne, 2011.

Broome, Richard, *Coburg: Between two creeks*, 2nd ed., Lothian, Melbourne, 2001.

Broome, Richard, *The Victorians: Arriving*, Fairfax, Syme and Weldon Associates, Sydney, 1994.

Brown-May, Andrew, *Melbourne Street Life*, Australian Scholarly Press, Melbourne, 1998.

Brown-May, Andrew and Swain, Shurlee (eds), *Encyclopedia of Melbourne*, Cambridge University Press, Monash University, first published in hardcopy 2005, www.emelbourne.net.au, multiple entries accessed December 2014–March 2015.

Buckrich, Judith, *Collins: The story of Australia's premier street*, Australian Scholarly Publishing, Melbourne, 2005.

Buckrich, Judith, *The Long and Perilous Journey: A history of the Port of Melbourne*, Melbourne Books, Melbourne, 2002.

Buckrich, Judith, *Melbourne's Grand Boulevard: The making of St Kilda Road*, State Library of Victoria, Melbourne, 1996.

Butler, John, *The History of St Kilda from its First Settlement to a City and After*, Printers Proprietary Limited, Melbourne, 1931.

Campbell, Alastair, *John Batman and the Aborigines*, Kibble Books, Melbourne, 1987.

Cannon, Michael, *The Land Boomers*, Melbourne University Press, Melbourne, 1966.

Carroll, Brian and Roger-Genersh, Arno, *Toorak and South Yarra Sketchbook*, Rigby, Adelaide, 1974.

Church, Julia, *Per L'Australia: The story of Italian migration*, Italian Historical Society, Melbourne, 2005.

Collingwood History Committee, *In Those Days: Collingwood Remembered*, Richmond Hill Press, Melbourne, 1979.

Coulson, Helen, *The Story of the Dandenongs*, Chesire, Melbourne, 1968.

Cunningham, Sophie, *Melbourne*, University of New South Wales Press, Sydney, 2011.

Cutten History Committee of the Fitzroy History Society, *Fitzroy: Melbourne's first suburb*, Melbourne University Press, Melbourne, 1991.

Darian-Smith, Kate, *On the Home Front: Melbourne in Wartime 1939–45*, Melbourne University Press, Melbourne, 2009.

Davison, Graeme, *The Rise and Fall of Marvellous Melbourne*, Melbourne University Press, Melbourne, 1978.

de Moore, Greg, "In from the Cold: Tom Wills – A Nineteenth Century Sporting Hero", PhD thesis, Victoria University, Melbourne, 2008.

Dennis, CJ, *The Songs of a Sentimental Bloke*, Angus & Robertson, Sydney, 1916.

Department of Transport, Planning and Local Infrastructure, *Vicnames Register of Geographic Names*, maps.land.vic.gov.au/lassi/VicnamesUI.jsp, multiple entries accessed September 2014–March 2015.

Dingle, Tony, *The Victorians: Settling*, Fairfax, Syme and Weldon Associates, Sydney, 1994.

Dunstan, David, et al, *Victorian icon: the Royal Exhibition Building Melbourne*, The Exhibition Trustees in association with Australian Scholarly Publishing, Melbourne, 1996.

Eidelson, Meyer, *Melbourne Dreaming: A guide to important places of the past and present*, 2nd ed., Aboriginal Studies Press, Melbourne, 2014.

Elsum, William, *The History of Williamstown*, facsimile edition, Craftsman Press, Melbourne, 1985.

Farrer, Vashti, "First Past the Post: The Melbourne Cup of 1861", Australian Dictionary of Biography, adb.anu.edu.au/essay/, accessed 1 January 2015.

Federation Square, *Federation Square Annual Report 2013*, www.fedsquare.com/wp-content/uploads/annual-report-june-2013.pdf, accessed December 2014.

Flannery, Tim (ed.), *The Birth of Melbourne*, Text Publishing, Melbourne, 2002.

Flannery, Tim (ed.), Morgan, John, *The Life and Adventures of Williams Buckley*, Text Publishing, Melbourne, 2002.

Ford, Olwen, *Harvester Town: The Making of Sunshine 1890–1925*, Sunshine and District Historical Society, Melbourne, 2001.

Gammage, Bill, *The Biggest Estate on Earth: How Aborigines Made Australia*, Allen & Unwin, Sydney, 2011.

Gibb, Don and Warmington, Stuart, *Visions of a Village: Canterbury Shops and Shopping 1880–1990s*, Canterbury History Group, Melbourne, 1995.

Harden, Michael, *Melbourne: The making of an eating and drinking capital*, Hardie Grant Books, Melbourne, 2009.

Heritage Victoria, *Victorian Heritage Register*, www.heritage.vic.gov.au, multiple entries accessed January–March 2015.

Heyward, Michael, *The Ern Malley Affair*, University of Queensland Press, St Lucia, 1993.

Hibbins, GM, *A Short History of Collingwood*, Collingwood Historical Society, Melbourne, 1997.

Kehoe, Mary, *The Melbourne Benevolent Asylum: Hotham's premier building*, Hotham History Project, Melbourne, 1998.

Lack, John, *A History of Footscray*, Hargreen Publishing Company, Melbourne, 1991.

Lang, Lisa, *EW Cole: Chasing the Rainbow*, Arcade Publications, Melbourne, 2007.

Lee, Jenny, *Making Modern Melbourne*, Arcade Publications, Melbourne, 2008.

Lemon, Andrew, *The Northcote Side of the River*, Hargreen Publishing Company, Melbourne, 1983.

Longmire, Anne, *St Kilda: The show goes on 1930–83*, Hudson Publishing, Melbourne, 1989.

McCalman, Janet, *Struggletown: Public and Private Life in Richmond*, Melbourne University Press, Melbourne, 1985.

Macintyre, S and Selleck, RJW, *A Short History of the University of Melbourne*, Melbourne University Press, Melbourne, 2003.

Marshall, Alan, *The Gay Provider: The Myer story*, Cheshire, Melbourne, 1961.

Melway Street Directory of Greater Melbourne, Melways, Melbourne, 1966–2008.

Moyes, Gordon, *When Box Hill was a Village*, ANZEA, Sydney, 1991.

Munro, Ian, "Overpaid, Oversexed and Over Here", the *Age*, Fairfax, Melbourne, 27 February 2002, accessed at www.theage.com.au/articles/2002/02/26/1014704950716.html, accessed January 2015.

Nepean Historical Society, www.nepeanhistoricalsociety.asn.au, multiple entries accessed January–February 2015.

O'Hanlon, Seamus, *Go! Melbourne in the Sixties*, Australian Scholarly Press, Melbourne Publishing Group, Melbourne, 2005.

O'Hanlon, Seamus, *Melbourne Remade: The inner city since the 70s*, Arcade Publications, Melbourne, 2010.

Otto, Kristin, *Capital: Melbourne when it was the Capital City of Australia 1901–27*, Text Publishing, Melbourne, 2009.

Otto, Kristin, *Yarra: A Diverting History of Melbourne's Murky River*, Text Publishing, Melbourne, 2005.

Peel, Victoria, Zion, Deborah and Yule, Jane, *A History of Hawthorn*, Melbourne University Press, Melbourne, 1993.

Penrose, Helen, *Brunswick: One History, Many Voices*, Victoria Press, Melbourne, 1994.

Power, Emily, *Fashion and Flemington*, Slattery Media Group, Melbourne, 2012.

Presland, Gary, *First People: The Eastern Kulin of Melbourne, Port Phillip & Central Victoria*, Museum Victoria, Melbourne, 2010.

Priestly, Susan, *South Melbourne: A History*, Melbourne University Press, Melbourne, 1995.

Priestly, Susan, *The Victorians: Making their Mark*, Fairfax, Syme and Weldon Associates, Sydney, 1994.

Prior, Tom, *Bolte by Bolte*, Craftsman Publishing, Melbourne, 1990.

Robinson, LM, *Madame Brussels: This Moral Pandemonium*, Arcade Publications, Melbourne 2009.

Rodriguez, Judith, *The Hanging of Minnie Thwaites*, Arcade Publications, Melbourne, 2013.

Rogers, Dorothy, *A History of Kew*, Lowden Publishing Company, Kilmore, 1973.

St Kilda Historical Society, www.skhs.org.au, multiple entries accessed September 2014–January 2015.

Sandringham Historical Society, www.sandringhamhistorical.com.au, multiple entries accessed September–December 2014.

Sands and MacDougall's Commercial and General Melbourne Directory, Sands and MacDougall, Melbourne, 1862.

Sands and MacDougall's Directory of Victoria, Sands and MacDougall, Melbourne, 1912–39.

Sands and MacDougall's Melbourne and Suburban Directory, Sands and MacDougall, Melbourne, 1863–1901.

Shaw, AGL, *A History of the Port Phillip District*, Melbourne University Press, Melbourne, 1996.

Sinclair, Jenny, *A Walking Shadow: The Remarkable Double Life of Edward Oxford*, Arcade Publications, Melbourne, 2012.

Sinclair, Jenny, *When we Think about Melbourne*, Affirm Press, Melbourne, 2009.

Sparrow, Jeff and Sparrow, Jill, *Radical Melbourne*, Vulgar Press, Melbourne, 2001.

Strahan, Lynne, *Private and Public Memory: A History of the City of Malvern*, Hargreen Publishing Company, Melbourne, 1989.

U'Ren, Nancy and Turnbull, Noel, *A History of Port Melbourne*, Oxford University Press, Melbourne, 1983.

Ward, Andrew & Associates, *Collingwood conservation study*, Collingwood City Council, Melbourne, 1989.

Wilde, Sally, *The History of Prahran*, Melbourne University Press, Melbourne, 1993.

Willett, Graham, Murdoch, Wayne and Marshall, Daniel (eds), *Secret Histories of Queer Melbourne*, Australian Lesbian and Gay Archives, Melbourne, 2011.

Wills, Elizabeth, *The Royal Exhibition Building, Melbourne*, Museum Victoria, Melbourne, 2003.

Yule, Peter, *Carlton: A History*, Melbourne University Publishing, Melbourne, 2004.

INDEX

ABOUT THE AUTHOR

For the last 15 years or so Dale Campisi has made it his business to get to know Melbourne. At first it was just to find the right bar, cafe or restaurant for this or that occasion, but the city got under his skin.

Melbourne is a city of stories. Dale got his first look into the city's past during his Australian history studies at university, and went on to uncover some of its lesser-known stories as publisher of Arcade Publications' little books about the city's colourful past. For a time Dale worked at the Public Record Office, and now he blogs about the city and leads regular tours for Melbourne Central and Hidden Secrets Tours. Over the years, he's written a number of travel guides to Victoria and Tasmania, most recently *Hide & Seek Hobart* and *Melbourne Precincts*. Dale does all this exploring with his partner Brady Michaels, whose photography illustrates this book. Soon they'll hit the road for a book about Australia.

ACKNOWLEDGEMENTS

Thank you to Jenny Lee for being such an inspiring mentor, colleague and friend over the years. Crucially she showed me that you can read the past in this city if you know where to look. Alice Barker has been a terrific editor to work with, and I hope I get to work with her again. Thanks too to Sarah Robins, Alison Proietto and Melissa Kayser for their support in the making of this book.

Acknowledgements

The publisher would like to acknowledge the following individuals and organisations:

Editorial manager
Melissa Kayser

Project manager
Alison Proietto

Editor
Alice Barker

Cartography advisor
Emily Maffei

Cover design
Josh Durham, Design by Committee

Internal page design
Peter Dyson @ desertpony

Layout
Megan Ellis

Index
Max McMaster

Pre-press
Splitting Image; Megan Ellis

Photography credits

Cover (left) Brady Michaels, (right) Juergen Hasenkopf/Alamy

*All other image*s © Brady Michaels, except:

Pages vii, 6, 10, 11, 13, 14, 15, 18, 19, 22, 26, 27, 28, 29, 30, 33, 35 (a), 36, 37, 38, 39, 42, 44, 47 (b), 48, 56, 63, 65 (b), 67, 70 (a), 71, 74 (a), 75, 78, 81, 82, 83, 84, 85 (a), 88, 90 (a), 93, 94 (a), 94 (b), 96, 98 (a), 99, 100, 102, 105 (b), 112, 114 (b), 115 (b), 116, 118–19, 120 (b), 125, 128 (a), 129 (a), 129 (b), 130, 132, 134 (b), 138 (b), 138 (c), 139 (a), 139 (b), 144, 146 (b), 147 (a), 148, 150 (a), 152, 153, 159 (b), 162, 170 (a), 171 (a), 174, 175 (b), 176, 179, 180 (a), 181 (b), 182 (b), 183, 184, 186, 188, 191 (b), 192 (b), 193, 196, 198 (b), 203, 204, 208, 212, 215 (a), 215 (b), 218, 222, 223, 224 (a), 224 (b), 226 (b), 227, 229, 230 (b), 232 (b), 233, 234 (b) State Library of Victoria Pictures Collection; 21 State Library of New South Wales; 40 (background) Pashabo/ Shutterstock.com; 97 (background) tankist276/Shutterstock.com; 97 Dmitri Ogleznev; 107 Neale Cousland/Shutterstock.com; 146 (background) elic/Shutterstock.com; 166 (a) & (b) Tracey Manallack Collection; 171 (background) Peter Dedeurwaerder/ shuttertsock.com; 185, 190, 201 Wikimedia Commons; 198 (background) Jeff Cameron Collingwood/Shutterstock.com; 200 Shack West; 216 National Gallery of Victoria.

Explore Australia Publishing Pty Ltd
Ground Floor, Building 1, 658 Church Street,
Richmond, VIC 3121

Explore Australia Publishing Pty Ltd is a division of Hardie Grant Publishing Pty Ltd

hardie grant publishing

Published by Explore Australia Publishing Pty Ltd, 2015

Form and design © Explore Australia Publishing Pty Ltd, 2015
Text © Dale Campisi, 2015

A Cataloguing-in-Publication entry is available from the catalogue of the National Library of Australia at www.nla.gov.au

Disclaimer
While every care is taken to ensure the accuracy of the data within this product, the owners of the data (including the state, territory and Commonwealth governments of Australia) do not make any representations or warranties about its accuracy, reliability, completeness or suitability for any particular purpose and, to the extent permitted by law, the owners of the data disclaim all responsibility and all liability (including without limitation, liability in negligence) for all expenses, losses, damages, (including indirect or consequential damages) and costs which might be incurred as a result of the data being inaccurate or incomplete in any way and for any reason.

ISBN-13 9781741174724

10 9 8 7 6 5 4 3 2 1

Printed and bound in China by 1010 Printing International Ltd

Publisher's note: Every effort has been made to ensure that the information in this book is accurate at the time of going to press. The publisher welcomes information and suggestions for correction or improvement. Email: info@exploreaustralia.net.au

www.exploreaustralia.net.au
Follow us on Twitter: @ExploreAus
Find us on Facebook: www.facebook.com/exploreaustralia